RUN GROW TRANSFORM

A Manufacturer's Guide to Digital Marketing

Stephen Fry
Michael Bird
Award Winning Digital Experts

SPIN VENTURES, INC.

Run Grow Transform, A Manufacturer's Guide to Digital Marketing

© 2016 Spin Ventures, Inc.

ISBN 978-0-692-76323-0

All rights reserved. No part of this book may be reproduced or transmitted in any form by any means, electronic or mechanical, including photocopying, recording or by any information storage and retrieval system, without permission in writing from the copyright publisher.

For information and distribution rights, royals, derivative works or licensing opportunities on behalf of this content or work, please contact Spin Ventures, Inc. at the address shown below or via email at info@RunGrowAndTransform.com.

COMPANIES, ORGANIZATIONS, INSTITUTIONS AND INDUSTRY PUBLICATIONS: Quantity discounts are available on bulk purchases of this book for reselling, educational purposes, subscription incentives, gifts, sponsorship or fundraising. Special books or book excerpts can also be created to fit specific needs such as private labeling with your logo on the cover and a message from the author printed inside. Contact Spin Ventures, Inc. at 877-225-4200 for more information.

Spin Ventures, Inc.
1370 NW 114th Street, Suite 300
Des Moines, IA 50325

This book was printed in the United States of America

Editor: Erin M. Fry
Cover and Icon Design: Jason C. LaCava
Formatting: Pamela J. Smith

Dedication

This book is dedicated to the leaders of manufacturing companies who still use old fashioned marketing techniques, but are willing to take a leap forward with digital. The rewards are worthy of the effort.

Acknowledgements

We take this opportunity to thank our wives, families, amazing team members at Spindustry, friends, business partners and most of all our awesome clients for making this book happen. Without their trust and support over the past 20-plus years, we couldn't possibly have the experience to share the ideas in this book.

Steve and Michael

Table of Contents

Acknowledgements vii
What is Digital? x
Introduction xi
The Digital Ecosystem xv

Section 1 – RUN Your Business 26
Reducing costs 28
Enhancing sales channel support 33
Determining what customers really want 37
Handling customer service in a better way 44
Communicating better with internal teams 48
Moving stale inventory 51
Working with old computer systems 54
Protecting the business' reputation 58
Keeping up with digital regulations 63

Section 2 – GROW Your Business 70
Finding and hiring great people 72
Looking at current marketing 77
Humanizing the brand story 80
Generating more quality leads 84
Selling more products and services 90
Expanding market share 100
Evaluating tradeshow investments 104
Monitoring the competition 109
Hiring internal people or a digital agency 114

Section 3 – TRANSFORM Your Business 120
Expanding into new markets 122
Adding direct-to-consumer business to a B2B model 126
Exploring international opportunities 131
Adding a subscription model 136
Transitioning to the next generation 140

About the Authors 144

What is Digital?

The word *digital* is widely used today but can have very different meanings. For the purposes of your exploration of this book, here's our definition.

> *Digital encompasses the use of the web, smartphones, email and social channels to connect businesses, products and people to one another in a real-time, relevant manner.*

Why should you care about digital marketing? Because digital marketing is reshaping how businesses communicate with customers, prospects and partners. If you're not yet at least experimenting with digital in your organization, you are putting the future of your company at risk.

This book will help you start the process of bringing digital marketing into your business for the first time or expand what you're already doing.

If you don't have time to read this book, give it to a designated leader in your organization who does and then listen to him or her when they come back to you with ideas.

Introduction

For the past twenty years, we've had the opportunity to work alongside a lot of companies. We've served some of the largest companies on the planet, some of the smallest and quite a few in between. At times our journey has been challenging—like in the early days having to educate our prospects and clients that the internet is for real—but for the most part it has been very rewarding and enjoyable.

So why are we writing this book? Simple. We love helping companies grow and become more efficient and it's frustrating to see great manufacturers missing out on opportunities to increase sales, attract new employees and innovate new products faster. If you own or run a manufacturing company and you follow the guidance we offer in the pages of this book, you'll see positive results. There are so many possibilities for manufacturing and distribution company owners and leaders to leverage the power of digital marketing to increase sales, improve margins and genuinely connect better with sales channel partners and end-consumers alike.

It is completely understandable, though, that for many companies, the idea of doing all of the things we describe in this book is just too overwhelming. If that sounds like you, we simply counsel you to take small steps. You can still find a worthwhile return by taking on only one (or a few) of the challenges that follow. If you need help, find a good digital marketing partner to lead your organization through the process.

We've designed this book to be easy for you to get through. We outline a number of common challenges that you may be facing. To make it simple to digest, you'll see that we group these challenges into three distinct areas of focus.

Run Your Business. If you're like most manufacturing company leaders, your top priorities come down to three basic things. The first is making certain that your *plant is operating efficiently*. The second is *giving your employees the tools they need* to do their jobs well. The third is *providing your channel partners and customers with the information* they need to select and buy the equipment you build.

In this section we'll take a closer look at some of the challenges typical manufacturing and distribution organizations face. We will also address how the digital world can bring an enhanced level of support, efficiency and cost savings to your business.

Grow Your Business. To be successful in today's business climate, you probably have a desire to grow your company. Your goals for growth may range from conservative to aggressive. Regardless, we'll outline a series of challenges you might be facing and then walk you through some ideas that you can put to use that will help you find growth and higher margins.

Transform Your Business. Moving beyond the business activities that are involved in running and growing a successful manufacturing organization, you may be looking to revolutionize or transform your business into something bigger—or different—than it is today. If you keep up with business and technology news, you know that our world continues to change ever more rapidly. It's likely that a lot of companies in business today won't be here in the future because they aren't evolving to meet the needs of their customers or to address new competitors that are disrupting long-standing business models and selling new products in new ways.

If you find one of these sections of particular interest, feel free to skip right to the challenges that are most relevant to you.

This book is intended to genuinely help you with your business. It's not like a lot of business books that simply impart knowledge; we want you to use this book and companion website at www.rungrowandtransform.com as an ongoing reference guide. The site will provide additional information about making your business stronger using digital strategies.

To make this book easier for you and your team to use, we're including a **1-in-30 Days Action Step** for each challenge. Each action step gives you one thing you can accomplish in the next thirty days to move forward with a particular challenge. Use the 1-in-30 action steps to help you explore what you're doing today and why, and then start to look at how you can implement positive changes going forward that will help your organization.

As a manufacturer, you face a myriad of challenges every day. Your industry may have more competitors than in the past. You may be struggling with sales channel partners who are nothing more than order takers. Perhaps finding new employees is a struggle for you. We'll address each of these concerns and a lot more. So, grab a note pad and let's get started. There's more high-margin business and cost savings out there if you're willing to follow the steps outlined in this book.

Good luck and let us know how you're able to grow your business leveraging digital!

The Digital Ecosystem

Before we dive into the business challenges and opportunities you may face as a manufacturer, we want to share more about the digital ecosystem. This section will serve as an active glossary of terms that we use throughout the book. First, we are defining different parts of the digital ecosystem, and then we discuss the process of creating digital assets like websites, landing pages, online ads, etc. Our hope is that this information will help orient you to what the digital ecosystem has to offer as you work with your team or with external digital experts.

A Little History

For many of you, your first experience with digital was likely an America Online (AOL) email account. Back then, email was little more than a complement to your phone, fax and in-person communication. Soon thereafter, email became a vital tool for doing business. The ability to communicate with friends, family and business associates expanded greatly. Then, websites emerged as the next step to being a part of the digital world. Originally, websites were viewed as the behind-the-scenes or unofficial newswire of a company, usually maintained exclusively by IT departments. Over time, however, we've seen websites evolve into the virtual front door of business.

As companies began getting comfortable with their websites—which took some time and compromise between IT and marketing—we saw social channels spring to life. Several different platforms were introduced, each of which urged companies to engage in this new communication style. These social channels gave companies the ability to provide more information and initiate an online discussion with their constituents for the first time. Not unlike websites, it has taken organizations a long time to fully embrace social media for the value it offers. Quite a number of companies, still today, are not taking advantage of social media, while others are doing nothing but the absolute basics.

Today, email, the web and social have all been accelerated into our lives with the use of smartphones. Gone are the days of dial up, though we recall, fondly, the cool telephone tones we heard as we logged onto the internet. Now, with the tap of a finger we can communicate with nearly any person or company on the planet 24/7. The expectation that a business listens and responds to their customers and sales channel partners has never been higher.

Today's Ecosystem

Websites, email and social media are just the tip of the iceberg of the digital ecosystem. There are many other important elements that make up the digital ecosystem. Here are some of the more important examples:

> *Microsites and Landing Pages.* While a microsite is a small website with a few pages and a landing page is typically just a single page, each serves the same general purpose. These websites provide niche content on the internet designed to attract potential customers. When used effectively, these sites are highly focused on a single idea and encourage visitors to take a directed, clear next step, like filling out a form, downloading a white paper, calling into a customer service or sales telephone number. You may have heard the term *content marketing*. This is simply the use of highly targeted information placed on a microsite, landing page or website that is designed to attract, educate and engage visitors (buyers), who need the exact product or service you offer. Microsites and landing pages are typically constructed at modest expense and the results derived from them can be measured with great accuracy.
>
> *Blogs.* A blog is a website used to post articles and opinions that are relevant to visitors. Blogs are generally

designed for one-way interaction with desired audiences. Unlike a discussion board that facilitates a cross flow of information between different parties, blogs are authored by organizational leaders and employees. For the purpose of sharing company information, the content of blogs should be written with a voice and tone that matches the personality of your company. While the content shared can certainly be business related, often the most effective blogs are those that showcase the personality and culture of a business. Sharing interesting stories about your company and your people or talking about the philanthropic efforts you support are examples of how blogs can be used. Readers can provide commentary, but with blogs there is much less back and forth interaction. Recognize that your blog content can often reveal a different and more humanizing perspective about your company than your main website.

Search Engines/Organic Search Engine Optimization. Search engines make it easy for people to find exactly what they're looking for online. The goal of search engine optimization is to make your content easy for the major search engines to find and index. You want your company to show up as one of the first organic results when prospects search in Google, Bing or Yahoo for the types of products you manufacture or distribute. Organic results don't cost you anything—you just have to continually do the right things to get your company to rank well. This goal is achieved in several ways, but it starts by having your website developer create a search-friendly infrastructure when building your website. As content is added, you'll want to make sure that it's filled with high-ranking keywords that match the phrases your prospective customers are typing into the search box. There is certainly more to it, but this is the basic idea.

Pay-per-click (PPC)/Google AdWords. In addition to ranking well in the search engines organically, you can *buy* your way to visibility. The easiest way to get to the top of the search engine results is to pay for clicks using Google AdWords. Other search engines also function in a similar manner. Yes, you'll have to pay when (but only when) an online visitor clicks on your company's listing, but if you want your company's products and services to be listed at the top of the results, you can. Best of all, unlike traditional advertising, you only pay for the visitors that click your ad, not everyone that sees your ad.

We hear some business leaders say that they think paid ads aren't as valuable as organic listings. The reality is that most statistics prove that thought to be wrong. People do click on paid ads, especially when the messaging of the ad is written in a highly relevant way that matches their needs. Savvy web users often do look at sponsored ads first, knowing that each company is paying to be there. If you need more proof, just look at how Google's stock has performed.

Well-designed and messaged banner ads that display on targeted websites can be a good way to reach prospective customers, dealers and employees who have an interest in the content offered. Creating paid content in "advertorial" format attracts online visitors who are looking for specific information about a product, service or challenge. Trade associations, industry sites and social media channels are all good places to display digital ads.

Stages of Web Development

A quick online search will provide a list of entire books written on various web development processes. Because that's not what this book is about, here is your crash course.

1. A good web development process will always begin with *strategy* and *goals*. A new website should not be built simply because you are bored with your current one. Before embarking on a new site, you need to review and understand what is and what is not working with your current site by reviewing your Google Analytics and other feedback you may have from visitors or your own team. To get good results, you really need to have documented, *quantifiable* business goals you want to achieve with the new site. Then, on at least a quarterly basis, check the progress of your site against the stated goals.

2. As a part of the strategic analysis process, you and your website developer should be identifying groups of customers and partners who will use the site. Focus on *why* these different types of visitors will use the site. These groups can be named different things, but the most common term we hear is *personas*. Regardless of what you call these groups, just make sure you identify them and know their specific business needs. A common challenge we see is that when thinking about a website, organizations view their content and story from the "inside-out" rather than from the "outside-in." To solve this, when writing any content for your website, put yourself in the shoes of your website visitors, who may not know your business or your internal jargon, and then imagine the questions they have or information they need to build a good relationship with your business.

3. After clarifying your quantifiable goals and the information that is needed to measure and support them, creating a site map is usually the next step. The site map will provide a high level "org chart" view of the eventual website and identify where different types of content will be housed.

4. With the site map completed, the next step is creating wireframes, or storyboards, for individual pages of your new site. Wireframes display page-level detail of the site map. The wireframing process will help your team see what elements need to be on each page. Having to make choices about what information goes on each page will force you and your team to think through your business processes and determine what different audiences want to see. Wireframing is typically an iterative process, meaning there is back and forth between the website designer and project sponsor as features and functions are evaluated and finalized. Plan on this work to take a few weeks—or longer for large websites—if you are doing it right. Using wireframes to determine functionality often saves money in the long run, because they minimize expensive programming rework.

5. Once you have approved the wireframes for your new website, the web designer will create a mock-up of one or more primary site pages. Most often the designer will create the home page and one inside page to demonstrate the look and feel of the new site. Additional mock-ups, sometimes called design comps, may be needed, depending upon the complexity of your new site. After any necessary revisions, full site design can begin.

6. With goals, a site map, wireframes and final design direction confirmed and approved, the creation of a website often then splits into multiple, concurrent paths.

Technical Design. A designer or, in some organizations, a programmer will need to take the approved mock-ups and wireframes and create HTML and other required technical files (CSS, JavaScript, etc.) that result in a website that can function on the internet.

Programming/Development. The programmer, sometimes called a developer, takes the HTML and associated files and connects them to databases or other sources of content. These technicians also develop interactivity, like forms, shopping carts and content management systems, which enable authorized people, including those who are non-technical, to add, edit and remove content on the website.

Content Team. With the final site map and wireframes in hand, your content team will have some idea what site content is needed. They can begin the process of gathering, curating or creating needed information, including text and images, before the site is fully developed. Typically, about midway through the development process, the content management system will be ready for your team to begin loading content. During this trial and error period, everyone can start to see how the new site looks with your company's content. Depending on budget, it may be more appropriate to have the development company's design team load at least the initial site content, as they can make sure each page looks good with your new site's overall design.

Search Engine Optimization ("SEO"). A separate team can be working simultaneously on *keyword research* and *content optimization*, which will help search engines find and index your content once it is live on your website. If you're going from an old site to a new site, you'll want to pay careful attention not to lose any of the search engine visibility you've already gained. Your team or your development partner can create what are called "redirects" to refer existing search engine results to new site pages. This SEO team will also work with the design and development teams to make sure that the structure of the new website will accommodate their needs to maximize search engine visibility.

Technical Support. Support technicians will be required to handle the final backend site needs and to configure the server(s) upon which your site will reside. Discussions surrounding the hosting of your site should have been a part of upfront planning. As development begins, hosting plans must be revisited to see if any of the initial assumptions have changed. There will be a checklist of other details to consider, depending on the type and complexity of the new site. For example, e-commerce sites and company intranets will require much more discussion.

7. As the new site nears completion, quality assurance and testing will intensify. We strongly recommend that testing be done throughout the design and development process to identify any issues long before they can become big problems. As the site starts to really take shape, it will be useful to move it from the development platform to a staging platform, where the site will not be in flux as developers and designers work on it. Note that even though you and your team can access the new site, it's not available to the public just yet. Immediately prior to the site's launch, final testing should be done in what's called the production environment.

8. It is important to perform retesting immediately after launch and then regularly for the first 30 days after launch and at least once or twice a year thereafter. This testing regimen will help minimize the likelihood of content abnormalities or unseen errors.

While not an exhaustive history of digital, glossary of all things internet or a manual on website development, we hope this overview helps you understand the complexities of the digital ecosystem. This information will align with our recommendations and allow you to make good decisions about hiring internal digital team members or engaging an external digital partner in the future.

Section 1
RUN Your Business

Section 1 – RUN Your Business

Run Your Business. If you're like most manufacturing company owners and leaders, your top priorities come down to three basic things. The first is making certain that your plant is operating efficiently. The second is giving your employees the tools they need to do their jobs well. The third is providing your channel partners and end customers with the information they need to select and buy the equipment you build. In this section we'll take a closer look at some of the sales and marketing challenges typical manufacturing and distribution organizations face and how the digital world can bring an enhanced level of support, efficiency and cost savings to your company.

We often see that *Running* issues aren't dealt with for the following reasons:

- Making changes affects your organization's daily activities, and people do not like change.
- Some issues, like making employees manually enter information into your computer systems multiple times, may not be a big priority for management or make a major impact to your bottom line.
- Evaluating how to incorporate digital technology and marketing into organizations requires careful thought and can be legitimately difficult.
- Unlike launching a new product or opening a new warehouse, digital enhancements to your business are not as exciting.
- Looking at these challenges and opportunities forces you to realize that your departments and facilities may not follow consistent policies and procedures. It can become easier to subconsciously stick your head back in the sand.

We could go on, but you get our point. While these realities are, indeed, real, there are many reasons to move ahead with the recommendations we're offering.

Unlike trying to *Grow* or *Transform* your business, in which ultimately the customer has to do or respond to something your business is doing, you can fully control your *Running* issues. We see management and team members who set goals that have external dependencies. Then, when the goals aren't achieved it becomes too easy to blame something or someone else. So, our recommendation is to take ownership of key *Running* goals and make their success dependent on you and your team, not your sales channel partners or your end customers.

We understand that sales and growth can be challenging. If 10% growth excites you, you should really appreciate the opportunity to save 10%. Why? Because savings is controllable and may even provide scalability that supports reinvestment in your growth goals.

While we know that change is hard, we hear employees often cite daily inefficiencies and "stupid" or "needless" processes as reasons they quit and move on to new opportunities. Ultimately, your team will appreciate it when they no longer have to enter data twice, troubleshoot the same problems over and over or operate without the information they need on a daily basis.

Section 1 – RUN Your Business

CHALLENGE:
Reducing costs
Most businesses look to reduce costs at some point. The really successful businesses make this a priority all the time. If you're interested in shaving some costs off of your books, you'll appreciate this look at how digital initiatives can help.

Using digital in your business will require an investment but the payoff can be substantial. There are numerous ways in which digital can make your business more efficient. Best of all, everything can be measured to enable realistic return on investment ("ROI") calculations.

As we always tell our clients, we don't advocate that technology should replace people, but that with technology your team can perform better and do more of the things that don't get done today. Depending on your business, there could easily be many more opportunities to reduce costs. Now we will share some of the cost savings we see in our work with manufacturers.

Communicating with partners. If you are still sending out physical mailings with printed materials, specs and price schedules, you might consider migrating some or all of this information online. If you're not ready to do this, you can at least pilot an experiment and see what feedback you receive. You will probably discover that your customers and partners appreciate that they can have access to up-to-date information online, all the time. The ability to be more nimble with real-time changes and the elimination of printing and postage costs has the potential to provide substantial savings to your business.

Traditional advertising. There is still a place for traditional advertising, but you should be carefully looking at whether the costs involved with phone book ads, tradeshows and trade magazines still make sense. We recommend to our clients that before cutting out these tactics completely, they ratchet their usage down incrementally to see what impact is felt. Run a smaller ad or have a smaller booth to see if this change causes any negative ramifications. In most cases it won't and you'll have savings you can invest in more modern, measurable marketing efforts. Another big advantage of digital marketing is that digital "artifacts" can live on indefinitely. Unlike the ad you place in a trade magazine, which has a finite lifespan, content in the digital world can be presented to new prospects and potential employees for as long as you like.

Eliminating duplicate entry. Here's an important insight that you probably know but may not give much attention to. Your team members *hate* having to enter the same information over and over into different systems, but it happens all the time. Not only is this kind of work painful for your team, it can really mess with your reporting and data integrity. Finding ways to simplify your data entry will make your employees happier, and the data you use to make decisions will be more accurate. We call that a win-win.

Collaboration across time zones. If you have people or customers in different time zones, especially internationally, digital can create opportunities for your employees to collaborate more easily and affordably. People can interact in real time or in online collaboration portals, which can be created to allow team members to work on their own schedule. When travel and communication hassles are reduced, you will have a team of workers in disparate locations that works better together, while minimizing labor costs.

Customer service efficiencies. Using online chat, email and Twitter to handle customer service needs can provide dramatic improvement in efficiency and customer satisfaction. For common requests, your customer service reps can handle multiple inquiries simultaneously using pre-canned responses that have been carefully reviewed in advance. It's not uncommon for a customer care professional to handle 3-5 times, or more, customer inquiries using these digital tools.

Printing Catalogs. Determining whether to continue printing catalogs or not is a common question for many of our clients. The answer depends on several factors. Most companies are scaling back on the production of catalogs, primarily because customers today are willing (and actually prefer) to go online to search for products and information. Sure, for some industries it still makes sense to produce catalogs, at least for now. The advantages of moving away from catalogs include the ability to display new products whenever they become available, remove products that are no longer available without having to wait until the next catalog run and, obviously, the printing and postage costs. Online catalogs can be easily customized to specific audiences, making them more relevant and effective at generating new business.

We are confident that there are some things you are doing in your business that could benefit from a digital review. For a long time we heard that eliminating catalogs was a no-go for many businesses, but now, a majority of customers appreciate the ability to do a criteria-based search for products and pricing in real-time, without having to lug around a big catalog. This is one example of many but it illustrates the point. Today, digital is often more acceptable and more desired than traditional methods of communicating. Don't be afraid to experiment with some of these ideas. You'll likely find that you'll save money in the long run and increase satisfaction on the part of your constituents.

Take some time to meet with your customer service people to see if they can identify any information they're having to enter twice (or more) to do their jobs. You'll probably hear several instances of this kind of duplication. If so, document the specific scenarios and investigate what can be done digitally to remedy these time wasters. If your customer service folks can't identify any duplication, they'll surely have other ideas on how to make their work more efficient.

Section 1 – RUN Your Business

CHALLENGE:
Enhancing sales channel support
Your sales channel is likely a vital part of your business. We'll review how you can elevate your communication to these important parties and get more good business from their efforts.

This is one of the most difficult challenges we'll cover in this book. The relationship between supplier and dealer, representative or wholesaler runs broadly from love to hate. Some manufacturers value their sales channel partners and are willing to do whatever it takes to keep their relationship on a happy, even keel. Others view their sales channel partners with disdain, loathing every interaction they have with one another. Unless you're ready to move to a direct-to-consumer sales and service model, we hope you have solid relationships with and are eager to support those independent businesses and people that are out there selling your equipment.

Depending on what kind of products you build, it is possible that with the internet you really don't need middlemen any longer. If that's the case, you're probably already moving in that direction. While it may be hard to purge the long-standing relationships of the past, the increased margins are very tempting. We can't counsel you on whether it's a good decision to disintermediate your business partners, but if that's your decision, you'll be excited to see what's possible when you're in control of a well-designed and well-executed digital sales model.

A possible hybrid model for those who aren't ready to completely give up on all of the sales channel partners is to keep the very best and get rid of the rest. In those areas where you have good dealers, continue to support them fully. If there are areas of the country or specific industries that you want to go after directly, you will want to have supportive relationships with your dealers and wind up your online efforts to attract and convert new B2C customers.

For those organizations that are not able or interested in changing the current indirect sales process, let's look at how you can enhance your relationships with sales channel partners. The long established rule that *people sell what they know* continues to be true. Your job is to make sure that your company is helping to educate your representatives at every turn. How? By offering easy-to-download product literature, sale sheets, product videos, specifications, training, customer details and more. Make sure that the dealers that represent your company have the latest information in whatever format they want. Don't make it hard for them to get this information. After all, you want them to really know your products.

The best companies generate and deliver sales leads to their channel partners by building lead generation websites that are designed specifically for each dealer. While there's an investment in creating these websites, the return is often staggering. If you make the investment in your dealer's business, they'll be more loyal to you—and they'll sell more for you.

You might cringe at this idea, but create an online forum to give your sales partners the easy ability to collaborate together. Let them ask questions of one another. They can help each other by sharing success stories and you'll be the beneficiary of additional sales.

A dealer portal is another important tool in developing and enhancing dealer relationships. These portals can save your internal support team a ton of time too. Through the portal, which requires valid login credentials, your dealers can access up-to-date inventory, pricing and order status information. They can also download ads, tradeshow schedules, new product demos and other training information. Dealers can also view their accounts and access a range of meaningful reports. Make sure that your dealer portal is designed for use on smartphones and tablets. Your dealers will love it when they can get to accurate, relevant information any time from anywhere.

Though the popularity of apps is waning with the widespread use of responsive websites, there are still good reasons to consider creating an app. One of the most important reasons is for your internal sales team or dealers who are frequently at locations that have no access to the internet. Another reason having an app might make sense is so your company is featured in the various app stores and to allow your information to be accessible via an icon on a phone (rather than having to go to a browser).

Finally, if your business requires multilingual communication, make sure that you support your dealers in those markets accordingly. You'll need to balance the investment with the need, but when you offer native language information to foreign dealers and their customers, you'll typically cultivate much deeper and more successful relationships.

If you are looking for new, more digitally-centered ways to support your sales channel partners, consider one or more of the ideas offered in this challenge.

1 IN 30

One of the biggest eye openers here is proving there is a problem. Contact five of your dealers anonymously and request product information. The probability that you will get out-of-date information or inconsistent information is high. If you discover this to be true, this should excite you about getting started on some of the ideas listed in this challenge.

Section 1 – RUN Your Business

CHALLENGE:
Determining what customers really want
Knowing your customers' preferences, desires and budgets are all critical factors to any business' marketing success. This isn't anything new, but when thinking about how your customers interact with your organization or sales channel partner, knowing how your customers want to engage is more important than ever. Not knowing could cost you a tremendous amount of money and goodwill.

While it may seem obvious that you should know your customer, we are often surprised at how little effort is made towards really understanding the people who purchase and use the products manufacturers build. Often most of the attention is focused on the products that an organization creates. While this is certainly an important function for any manufacturing business, understanding your end consumers—those who ultimately buy and use the products you make or distribute—is critical to growing your organization successfully.

If your team already has a strong understanding of the types of customers you serve, consider yourself fortunate. It's surprisingly rare. If you don't feel you have a quantifiable understanding of your customers, to the point of creating personas for each, here are some guidelines to help you get started.

Categorize products/customers. Spend some time categorizing your products into their various uses. Are there different kinds of customers who use your products? If so, make a separate list for each. The differences will span demographics—old, young, professional, male, female, Caucasian, African American, Midwesterner, Southerner; income—lower, middle and upper; industrial customer or retail customer; traits like technology user—first adopter, late adopter, etc. The more refined you make your list, the more value you will derive from this effort.

Persona names. Once you have identified your customer types, give a specific name to each type. For some this is a strange approach but trust us, it will help your team get into the mindset of your customers at a deeper level once they can identify them as a specific person. You might have a few customer personas or you may have many. Whatever makes sense for your organization is fine.

Understand the personas. Now that you have identified and named your personas, start noting what they do that is of interest to your business. If, for example, you manufacture mattresses, it would be important to know:

Are they living in a home or apartment?

Where do they research purchases? Google? Friends? Manufacturer websites? Consumer sites? Magazines?

What triggers their desire to purchase a new mattress?

Is their current mattress old?

Have they recently moved into a new place?

Are they upsizing?

Are they dealing with back problems?

Are they buying for a child?

Where do they typically buy their mattresses? Department store? Furniture store? Discount warehouse? Online?

Getting granular. This is just a small sampling of the type of customer detail you need to be able to make smart marketing decisions, but you get the idea. Once you have this kind of information, you can quickly determine whether a specific marketing tactic is apt to make a positive impact or not. While it is unlikely that we would ever advocate the elimination of traditional advertising methods altogether, we do like digital marketing because of its ability to get so granular. You can advertise to target audiences that align perfectly with your personas, crafting messages that are ideal for each. Best of all, you can test and retest concepts in real time to see which are most effective. Over time you keep doing more of what works and eliminate those actions that aren't performing as well.

When we talk about performance, it's often sales but it doesn't have to be. Let's change gears a bit and look at a manufacturer of industrial equipment--perhaps equipment that costs tens of thousands of dollars and involves a lengthy sales cycle. Selling this kind of equipment online may not be realistic. Does that mean you shouldn't use digital channels to market these goods? Absolutely not. To the contrary, following the same model we described with the mattress manufacturer, you need to create personas for the buyers of your industrial equipment.

Just like the buyer of a new mattress, the industrial buyer will gather information from one or more sources. Today it's often Google or one of the other search engines. Give interested prospects the opportunity to download a whitepaper on the benefits of using your company's equipment or an online case study that shows how the use of a specific apparatus saved one of your clients a lot of time or money.

Once you know how your target audience's buying process works, you can generate content or applicable search engine marketing to drive ideal prospects to your products first and then to your internal team or sales partners to begin a relationship. Rather than a sale, the ROI measurement may involve conversions of online visitors to a case study download.

Any portion of the sales process may be supported by online efforts.

There's no doubt that some businesses still exist outside the confines of the internet, but this number is shrinking all the time. On still too many occasions we hear executives talk about how they just don't think that their website is that important to their business. This might be true, but how do you know? A great way to find out is to visit with your customer service team. Ask why people are calling in. Often, you'll hear that prospects first visited your website (which is available 24/7). If you really want to know, set up a unique toll-free telephone number and place that number exclusively on your website. Then, have your customer service team track the number of calls they get to that number. Even if your company doesn't sell equipment online, you may be surprised at how often your website plays a role in your end customer's decision making process.

There are certainly other ways you can learn about your customers. Let's review some other methods for gathering this information.

> *Learn from your employees.* Look to your own people. Sit down with your receptionist, inside sales and customer service teams to learn the reasons people are phoning your company. Better yet, listen into an afternoon of calls yourself. Are there consistent questions that come up time and time again? Perhaps clarifying the messaging on your website, literature or packaging will reduce call volume. Your customer service team may also have a good list of suggestions from your customers. Encourage your team to always be open to feedback from the people who use your products. This is true for all industries and customer types. The findings you get from this exercise may lead to new products, product enhancements or completely new uses (markets) for the products you manufacture or distribute.

Website search terms. Hopefully you track what people type into your website's search box. This information will provide you and your marketing team with an amazing amount of insight. Repeatedly, we find that our clients learn things from this analysis, like new nomenclature, because what you call your products isn't necessarily what your customers call them. Other insights might include different spellings for your products, a need for something you don't already have or the realization that people just can't find content that's actually on your site. In any of these cases you'll learn how to better communicate with your customers and, if the issues are addressed, will lead to greater profit margins.

Website analytics. Like the search box, your website analytics will provide an amazing amount of information about how people find and use your website, from what sites they came and more. When set up correctly, Google Analytics will generate incredibly valuable customer insights. But, you have to take the time to look at this data and either learn how to interpret it yourself or find someone who can provide guidance on what you're seeing and how to take action based on this information.

Online survey. It's possible that even with well documented customer personas you will still have questions about your end customers and their buying process. In that case, you might want to turn to an online survey to ask your website visitors or current customers to share information. From our experience, you'll get a far higher response rate if you limit your questions to no more than three or offer a nice incentive to complete something longer. If you ask just right, you'll be surprised at the amount of great information you can get.

We can't emphasize it enough. You need to really know and document your customers to maximize the value of any marketing. This is particularly true for digital marketing. Those companies that take audience identification seriously and do it well are highly rewarded with happier customers, sales partners, internal team members and higher revenues and profit. This stuff really does work.

1 IN 30

Find out whether Google Analytics tracking is set up on your website properties. Then, make sure you have someone who really understands this data and have them walk you through it to prove that it is configured properly on your website properties. Also, if there is a search function on your website, ask to see what people are searching for and, importantly, what results they are receiving. Having these two sources of data is a great first step to better knowing your customers.

Section 1 – RUN Your Business

CHALLENGE:
Handling customer service in a better way
Even assuming you have a great customer service team, your end consumers and sales channel partners want more self-service options for accessing information from you. Let this growing group of people get what they want, when they want it and you'll have a more loyal following.

While some people still like to talk to a human, a growing majority are tired of complex phone trees that are prevalent today. These folks want to be able to self-serve their customer service issues. Let's take a look at how you can handle both of these types of people.

Looking for Interaction. For those who want to have interaction with one of your customer service representatives, add an economical online chat feature to your website. What's great about these tools is that once trained, a customer service rep can handle multiple conversations at once. Also, because most inbound chat requests will be about similar things, it's easy to build an online database of well written responses. This will help make it easier for your rep to handle questions and make sure that the answers the visitors receive are consistent.

If you have sales channel partners who are looking for guidance or customer service and you happen to have enough staff, it's a good idea to establish specialized customer service reps who handle these "internal" requests for information. Make your dealers feel special by providing timely and accurate customer service and they'll buy more from you.

Another way to provide good customer service is to have your best reps respond to inbound requests from Facebook and Twitter. These social channels are becoming more popular for quick, transactional issues and for urgent matters.

Self-Service, Please. There's a growing population that hopes to never have to actually talk to anyone on your company's phone lines. They want to get online, get their issue resolved and then move on. The idea of having to stumble through a recording of your company's extensions may drive them to a competitor that offers online customer service. This is a big deal—and getting bigger all the time. If you don't believe us, look around the next time you're out in public. The smartphone is taking over communication and patience is in shorter supply than ever.

One way to support your customers is to offer online education and training. This is true whether you're selling to dealers or end users. If people want to view some training or learn how to use your product in a short video series, give them that option. They'll value your company for making it easy for them to get what they need. Over time, you'll have great cheerleaders for your business.

You might also consider offering your end consumers the ability to register their warranty online. Not only can you gather the information you need to track warranty issues, but even if you don't sell equipment directly (your dealer does), you will now have the end customer's information.

Once you know your customers by name and email, you can proactively send offers on their birthday, anniversary or other desired, personalized occasions. We don't advocate alienating your sales channel partner, but you may be able to grow your business by connecting with the people who use the products you make. Building this list is one of the most valuable ways to protect your interests should your relationship with a dealer ever go awry.

If you are sending correspondence directly to your end consumers, one of the ways you can be most relevant is to segment your customers into groups and leverage that information to your benefit. Doing this will allow you to show product photos that match what they currently have or need. You'll validate that you understand your customer when the information you send them shows imagery of their exact product in the background.

If you don't have any segmentation applied to your customer emails, then your first step is to begin that process. This can be done by running your email list through a classification program. With each new email you send, use a survey to ask a simple, easy-to-answer question. As responses come in, start dividing your list into appropriate buckets. You may have to ask a series of questions, but once you get your lists aligned, you'll be in a better position to market your equipment effectively.

Most electronic newsletter tools will track which news article or promotion each user clicks. This information can then be used to assist in the segmentation process. With these divided lists in hand, you can provide proactive ideas for maintenance and replacement part purchasing. These tactics will help build a strong relationship with your customers. They will come to appreciate that you have their best interests in mind when every communication they receive from you is timely, relevant and helps them use your product effectively.

Even if you rely on channel partners to sell your equipment, you can still have a relationship with your end customers. By having regular communciation with these users, you can listen to their ideas, which may generate new products, new configurations, new ways to sell and more.

Customer service models are changing as customers are often willing to self-serve their needs. You can empower your existing customer service team with online tools to make their job easier and deliver a better experience for your customers.

Get a good understanding of how your customer support is handled today. You may underestimate the number of emails and phone calls that happen in a day. The percentage of each may also surprise you. If you don't have a good grasp of this information, it should be pretty easy and painless to get. Assuming you have this data and the volume of inquiries is a problem, installing chat software is easy and inexpensive. Be sure not to overpromise new service levels to your customers out of the gate. You don't have to offer 24/7 chat, for instance, but add this tool to your website and look at the interactions over the next 90 days to evaluate its long term benefit to your business.

Section 1 – RUN Your Business

CHALLENGE:
Communicating better with internal teams
Your employees are the lifeblood of your business and replacing them is expensive and time consuming. We'll show you how the best companies leverage digital to stay in close contact to build long-term employee relationships.

Positive communication with your employees is more important than ever before. Many companies have team members who are dispersed across multiple locations, like the company headquarters, regional offices, client facilities, coffee shops, cars and home offices across the country or in the far corners of the world. Staying connected to your entire employee group ensures that you're able to share and receive the information you need. Having a digitally-based communication channel gives each employee a sense of being a part of the organization.

How are you communicating with your workforce today? Hopefully you're using at least some of the modern, digital tools that give your employees access to HR information, policies and procedures and up-to-date news about the company. As a starting point, most manufacturers have some kind of an intranet today, a web-based (or cloud-based) system that is the daily online starting point for accessing company information. If you don't have an intranet yet, make that a priority. Do it correctly. By that we mean, have a plan for what types of documents, data and information you will provide and determine what common nomenclature to use for the content areas of your intranet. Have people assigned to review and load content on a regular basis so your new intranet doesn't become a dumping ground.

If you want your workforce to strive towards a common company vision then your intranet is the perfect place to remind every employee, every day of their specific goals and how they align to the overall vision. Your company intranet can be used to display graphs, charts and other types of visual information that quickly convey to your team members know how they're contributing to the company's goals.

To get people using the intranet daily, don't hesitate to display stuff that has little or nothing to do with work, like birthdays, work anniversaries, upcoming events and even internal classified ads. Anything that you can do to have your team checking the intranet is a good thing.

One of the tactics we find most valuable in building intranet solutions is calling attention to recently added content. When an employee logs into the intranet today, make sure that anything new that's been posted since they last logged in is highlighted in some way. Otherwise, it's hard for them to know what's new, if anything.

Be sure and give your team an opportunity to provide feedback on the company intranet. You need to clarify what kind of information you're seeking. You might want their thoughts on your business operations as a whole, or you may want to limit responses to the intranet itself. You will surely appreciate the good ideas you receive from this feedback channel.

Another way to communicate with your own work force is to post engaging pictures and stories on social channels. Facebook, being common and widely used, is a good place to start. Show off your company's personality with some pictures of your team's volunteering efforts or work on a special project. Make the pictures and the story fun, but do not embarrass anyone. Your team and their friends and families will appreciate the recognition of being featured on your company's social media platforms.

Leveraging digital tactics in the right way will facilitate communication that's more efficient and effective, leading to greater job satisfaction and reduced employee turnover.

1 IN 30

The next time your company has something important to announce, keep track of the primary method used to communicate the message.

Then, a day or two after your announcement, touch base personally with a cross section of your team to see if they know about the news. Think about someone who will start as a new employee 30 days from now. Assuming your latest announcement is relevant to their job, how will they learn this information? Do you have a training handbook? If so, will this latest announcement be added to it? Based on your findings, consider the ideas presented in this challenge as strong methods to shore up any gaps in communication.

Section 1 – RUN Your Business

CHALLENGE:
Moving stale inventory
If you have old inventory that is taking up precious space, move it and make a nice profit.

In our work we find a lot of manufacturers that have a stockpile of old inventory collecting dust. It may still be on the books as an asset, but everyone knows that its real value is pretty minimal. You may need to hold on to this inventory to meet the occasional needs of customers with old equipment. If so, that's a cost of doing business. If you'd rather find a way to move these items and make some money in the process, we have some ideas you can consider.

An initial question is determining who might want the old inventory you have. Is this old inventory useful only to the people who own your products? If so, perhaps you can notify your dealers of a specially priced set of inventory, available on a first come, first served basis. You can go direct-to-consumer and offer a clearance sale on your website. The cost of carrying inventory over a long time might mean it makes sense to offer substantially discounted prices for these items. Remember, the likelihood of selling your old parts and pieces will increase exponentially if you have a well written description of each item and accompany the words with clear, detailed photos. If there are other uses for these items, write descriptions for those as well. You can also turn to online auction sites, like eBay, to move these kinds of products.

Another option for selling stale inventory is to bundle products together. Instead of selling one or two of the items at a time, try packaging 50 or 100 in a set. Offer a good price and you may be able to reclaim valuable shelf space.

One of our favorite ways to move old inventory is by creating a continuity program. If your buyers need these items on a regular basis or if you have enough products that are different but valuable, try selling a subscription that gives buyers a package of these goods, delivered once a month.

Different types of inventory can dictate unique ideas for getting products out the door. Hopefully you can use one of these approaches to get that old stuff paid for and off your hands.

1 IN 30

Stop stalling. If you have old inventory sitting around your warehouse, go take some pictures of it and put a listing on eBay, maybe two. One listing could cover a small quantity of products and the other could show the entire lot. Think about the words or phrases a prospective buyer would type into Google to get to your products and then be sure to include those in your description. Remember, you only need one person in the whole world to be searching for what you have. People are looking for obscure things every minute of every day. Similarly, if you have a segmented email list with a group that could be interested in your overstock, don't overthink it. Send them a quick email and let them know you are open to "best offer" bids and see what happens.

Section 1 – RUN Your Business

CHALLENGE:
Working with old computer systems
An older IT system (often referred to as a legacy system) can have many ill effects on your business. It can limit choices and allow technology to drive your future rather than your business goals. Legacy systems also encourage silos of data to emerge when the old system cannot be updated to track new information. Having important data in places your IT team doesn't know about is common and could be costing you a lot of money. Let's look at how you can reduce the likelihood that your company's data is at risk.

If your business has mission critical technology systems that were built back in the 1970s or 1980s, you're not alone, but you are at risk. If your organization relies on legacy technology to manage its day-to-day information, this can pose a significant challenge when it comes to embracing modern, digital technologies. The hurdles are often surmountable but there will be effort and expense involved.

We recognize that changing an old system usually requires a large investment, and can take many months or even years of planning, implementation and training. Our focus in this challenge is based on the reality that your outdated system cannot be changed in a timely manner. You need a workaround to allow your business to move forward with modern websites and other digital initiatives needed for today's successful marketing mix.

The first thing is to determine whether your legacy system is "open," meaning it can export and import data. As an example, let's imagine you have all of your product data in a legacy ERP system that you want to display on your website. Let's then imagine that your old system doesn't allow any direct access to its product data. Why would it? Back in 1982, when your ERP system might have been created, your predecessor wanted a fully secure system. Websites were still 10-plus years away at that time.

So what do you do? Clearly, you would rather not have to

have all of your product information re-entered into the website's content management system. That would be a monumental undertaking, for sure. If your legacy system can export product data, then your team can import it into your website. That said, you may need to have your ERP expert or your experienced web development team create "web only" data about each product for use on your website. This information, which might include longer descriptions, images, and related information about products, may not currently be housed in your legacy system.

Another way you can look at this process is to imagine that your plant burned to the ground last night. We know that's a terrible thought, but for the sake of planning, it could happen. If nothing made it out of the fire, what information has your IT team backed up? And, perhaps more importantly, what information was not backed up? Knowing what data is lost will help reveal the hidden systems that exist in your business today.

Building a website is often the activity that causes your IT team to do a complete data inventory. When you think about the content your new website needs, you'll see that your legacy system probably plays a major role. But as you dig deeper, you may find that some of the information you wish to display on your website is stored in various "silos" throughout the departments of your business. Customer warranty information might exist in an Excel spreadsheet in your customer service department, subscriptions to your service plan might be stored in an Access database in your service department, and you may learn that your accounting system has no interaction with any of these other information sources.

While it's possible that your legacy systems may not allow the storage of all of your company's important data in one place, once you know where all of your data is housed, your website can be used to shelter most, if not all, of this information. In this way, you can reduce the likelihood that data is stored in unknown places around your company and make sure that it gets backed up on a regular basis. In the process of consolidating much of these outlying information assets into a single, web-based platform your IT team may well discover the opportunity to update some of your business processes at the same time, potentially saving you a lot of money.

Even if your business does not have multiple facilities, ponder these possibilities when looking at a new system or re-examining the future plan of an old one.

1 IN 30

Tackling the flow of information through your entire organization is the first step, but it can be daunting. Consider the "sore thumb" principle and try to eliminate one silo of information. We've rarely found a company that doesn't have vital information stored on someone's desktop or laptop. It just happens. Have your IT team perform an audit to determine where your important data is stored. At least then you'll know what you are dealing with. It could be relatively minor or it could be that you need to implement aggressive changes to protect your business.

Section 1 – RUN Your Business

CHALLENGE:
Protecting the business' reputation
Your business' reputation is at risk. Even one dissatisfied person can wreak havoc on how people see your company online. We'll give you some tips on how to monitor and manage your leadership team's and business' reputation.

In the pre-internet days, managing your business' reputation was fairly straightforward. Unless your company was doing something bad enough to get on the news, the likelihood that many people would find out about a problem was negligible. In today's world of social media and online blogs, however, a single disgruntled customer can cause real public relations damage to your business by spreading their one-sided frustrations to their friends and their friends' friends at exponential speed.

Not only can your business be subjected to extreme public scrutiny when someone chooses to go on a public, online rant, your employees and management team members can be called out for things they've done—sometimes outside of work. Social media has certainly blurred the lines between our work and personal lives. If one of your team members does something inappropriate in their personal lives, your company could face unexpected repercussions.

If you're not prepared for the realities of today's offended customer or angry ex-employee, you could be in for a rude awakening. We have seen firestorms caused by relatively small actions that set off one or more people. What's worse, the controversial messaging, which could be a blog article, a Facebook post or even a video on YouTube, can start taking over your search engine results.

Imagine you've worked hard to get your company ranked well for the products and services you offer. Then one day an unhappy customer or even someone who has never done business with your organization takes to the internet to proclaim how your company has mistreated them. Suddenly, that content starts to rank in some instances *better* than your own company's information in the search engines. So, when your customers and prospects are checking out your business, they see results showing your company in a bad light. It's not pretty and it can be very difficult to clean up this kind of bad review.

There is another set of issues that we've seen arise when an inexperienced employee, often an intern, is put in charge of your company's social media. Sometimes it can be an innocent misunderstanding that leads to people thinking that your company is in chaos. Think about that for a minute. You've invested your life in building a great company and it all comes down to the innocent slip up of an inexperienced employee who meant well but has created a giant mess for you to clean up with the public. If you think back to when you were first joining the workforce, would your boss have ever given you a microphone to share the company's message to the world?

Worse than the innocent mistake is the employee who has unpopular (or offensive) beliefs and will stop at nothing to share his or her feelings, even on the company's social channels. Twice in the past few years we've seen some sizeable companies forced to engage expensive public relations firms to help diffuse situations like this. In one case, the individual involved was a summer intern that went on a racist rant on a corporate Facebook page. In the other instance, it was an employee who was unhappy about the way the company was doing business.

Now, if your company is actually engaging in improper things, like mistreating people or taking advantage of customers, you're going to have to deal with the consequences. What we're talking about are those situations where the claims are completely false or based on honest mistakes. When your business or team members are working hard to serve customers and still get a bad rap, that's when your frustration level will skyrocket.

So how do you combat these situations? The first step is knowing that they exist. That means carefully monitoring the web and your social channels so you know what's being said about you, your business and your team members. If you haven't set up Google Alerts for your company and executive team, that's a good first step. Beyond that, one of the things you should do is spend some time reviewing the social media channels in which your company participates. There are a host of reputation monitoring services that can scan for your company more broadly to find what people are saying. If your business tends to have controversial interactions with customers or the community then subscribing to one of these services is a must.

Generally, we recommend that our clients allow negative commentary to stay (rather than delete it), because it gives you the ability to be genuine and answer concerns quickly and reasonably. Companies that redact any negative commentary are viewed as cold and impersonal. If you're in business, you're occasionally going to have to deal with people who are unhappy. Rather than push them aside, the best companies openly address the concerns and demonstrate to the community at large how you handle things when your team slips up.

If you, your employees or your company are being accused of something you didn't do, that may require a different approach. One option is to simply be nice, respond with compassion and then let it go. If you really think it's worth the battle, you can address the complaint and share your side of the story. While the public is quick to defend the customer who is terribly wronged, they also understand that some people are never happy and just complain to get attention. Our guidance when dealing with a negative situation is to share a neutral public response and then take further discussion with the individual offline.

One of our clients operates a giant retail store. A secret shopper visited the store and had a bad experience, leading to a poor review. We were able to notify our client that this secret shopper, who has a large online following, had posted a harsh recap of his visit. Rather than sweep the news under the rug, our client chose to face the situation head on. They invited the shopper back to the store and gave him a VIP tour. The result was a follow up review that spoke highly of the retailer. While the negative review was never removed, the community saw that the retailer cared and took steps to remedy the problem.

Handling your business' reputation is more important than ever because of the damage that can occur so quickly by so few. Make it a priority to keep an ear to what people are saying about your company in social media channels, blogs, forums and video channels, like YouTube. Once you know what's being said about your organization, you can determine how to best respond to commentary.

1 IN 30

Set up those Google Alerts. We have all "Googled" ourselves or our company name but that is different than setting up alerts and getting an email daily or weekly as things about you or your company are mentioned online. You can do this for your competitors as well. While you may eventually evolve to more sophisticated ways of doing this kind of monitoring, this is a good start.

Simply search online for "Google Alerts," login and set up alerts on your company name, key staff members and brand names for your products and services. Depending on the amount of activity, you can choose whether to move to a more sophisticated monitoring approach.

Section 1 – RUN Your Business

CHALLENGE:
Keeping up with digital regulations
There's no question that doing business online is complicated. You need to be aware of some important requirements today and realize that more are coming soon. We'll share some details on compliance that you need to know.

Digital brings so many great advantages to manufacturing and distribution companies, but the requirements that accompany the many benefits are both important and sometimes complex. The first realization is that the digital world is in a state of constant change. If you are unwilling to invest in the necessary resources to follow and interpret new requirements and laws, then you could be in for a rough ride.

Security challenges are one of the driving forces behind the everchanging digital landscape. Because of a relatively few number of people who have a desire to steal information and otherwise cause damage online, we all have to cope with new software and infrastructure changes on a consistent basis. Passwords need to be changed, web browsers get updated by their providers, data management requirements evolve and much more. Here is a review of the things you need to think about every day.

> *Data management.* Your list of customers and the information you have about them is among your business' most valuable asset. In our work we see too many companies that are lax about locking down access to this valuable data. Make sure that your customer information is accessible only to those people that need to see it. Don't make it easy for a bad employee to make a copy of your confidential information only to share it with a competitor. Take the time now to manage your data

appropriately and you can minimize the risks of having costly issues later.

Web browser changes. Until recently, it was common for web browser versions to change on a regular basis. This meant that your web team had to reconfigure your website, blogs and other online assets to work well with newer web browsers on a regular basis. Sometimes the modifications necessary were simple and other times they required a lot of work.

Security concerns have led to new browser plans that include having only one supported version at a time. This change is actually a good thing for your business, because it eliminates the hassle and expense of keeping your web assets tuned for many browser versions. There are still multiple browsers available, like Chrome, Firefox and Opera, but soon they will each have only one supported version at a time.

Payment Card Industry ("PCI"). Compliance to credit card transaction rules is a big deal. Hopefully your company is not storing customer credit card information on your servers. If you are, you need to address this quickly or risk substantial liability if someone with malicious intent breaks into your company's servers. These standards were created for the protection of all transactions that involve payment cards. The compliance requirements cover the period during and after an online purchase. The rules are complex but our basic guidance is that you *never* want to capture or store any kind of payment card information on your servers. There are payment gateways that will seamlessly handle that part of e-commerce for you, protecting you from risk of data theft. If you do any online commerce, get with someone who has PCI compliancy knowledge and make sure your company is doing things correctly.

Health Insurance Portability and Accountability Act ("HIPAA"). If your business has any transactions related to health care, including employment related health information, HIPAA may affect you. Similar to PCI compliance, HIPAA is designed to restrict access to an individual's health care information. Like PCI, the penalties for failing to comply with HIPAA requirements can be severe, so this is certainly something to pay close attention to in your business. If you're unsure of your company's situation you may want to have an external audit performed to evaluate what you're doing today and what potential liabilities you face, so you can take prompt corrective action.

CAN-SPAM Act. If your business uses email, you need to be aware of the CAN-SPAM Act. The requirements extend beyond bulk email to all commercial email. There is a long list of rules involved in compliancy, but the main requirements are that recipients must proactively want to receive emails from you and, when they no longer wish to receive your emails, you must give them the opportunity to easily remove themselves from your company's mailing list. There are significant fines in the U.S. and even stricter rules and penalties if you send emails to individuals in Canada.

Americans with Disabilities Act ("ADA"). We find that few people are talking about ADA, but believe they will soon. When the Americans with Disabilities Act was signed into law back in 1990, the internet wasn't commercially available. While there are no current ADA compliance requirements for websites, it looks like they are coming. Providing equal access to your company's online content to disabled visitors (who use, for example, screen readers to listen to website content being read aloud) is likely to become a legal mandate in the not too distant future.

In our experience, the majority of companies are still largely unaware of the ADA standards or have chosen to ignore them. Numerous companies have been sued already because of their website's lack of access to those with disabilities. Most always, these suits are settled out of court for substantial sums. New rules were scheduled to take effect in 2014, but those have been delayed.

There's still much uncertainty about what will be required and by what date, but currently it is expected that most, if not all, companies will be required to comply with website ADA standards sometime in 2018. Those organizations that choose not to make the necessary site modifications may face large fines and other penalties, just like those companies that chose not to update their physical facilities back in the 1990s.

Development Platform Changes. You know that technology changes regularly. The same is true of the underlying programming languages that are used to develop online properties, like websites, blogs and e-commerce sites. As new security and usability standards evolve, developers need to upgrade the tools they use to build things for the web. This means that at some point all web applications will run their lifecycle. When the tools become outdated and no longer supported, you'll need to invest in upgraded technology platforms. This doesn't mean you have to rebuild a web property, though you might, depending on the significance of the changes. Just be aware that, like much of your factory equipment, things evolve and need to be upgraded.

Like your HR, accounting and legal matters, it's good to have digital experts available to help you monitor your compliance to the changing requirements involved in interacting in the online world. While there are real expenses associated with this ongoing analysis, these costs pale in comparison to the fines that can be levied against your company if you're found to be in violation of these laws.

1 IN 30

Get a quick audit of your compliancy in place. Talk to your web team and ask them to document how they're currently handling credit card transactions. If they indicate that they're storing credit card information, that's a huge red flag that you need to address. If you're conducting e-commerce, talk to your marketing department about how they're managing your company's email lists. For example, if your organization is sending emails to Canada and there's violation, you could risk a fine of thousands of dollars per email sent.

Section 2
GROW Your Business

Section 2 – GROW Your Business

Grow Your Business. To be successful in today's business climate, you probably have a desire to grow your company. Your goals for growth may range from conservative to aggressive. Either way, we'll outline a series of challenges you might be facing, and then walk you through some ideas that you can put to use to help you find growth and higher margins.

Between *Running*, *Growing* and *Transforming*, we imagine you spend the most time thinking about the growth of your business. Even though growth is top of mind, most business leaders tend to focus on the same solutions year after year to increase sales. Too many companies seem to run out of steam after the first quarter when things don't go as planned. We are confident that the following digital ideas will help your company grow:

- Using digital tactics can help your team meet their sales and growth goals.
- Almost all sales people despise tracking their activities. Digital tools that alert and remind your sales team may help them stay on track.
- Digital tools and alerts can also help provide visibility to management, so you can stay in closer touch with your sales team.
- Digital marketing can generate new leads for your sales team to close.
- Using digital tactics will help you learn more about your channel partners and end customers, which will better equip your sales people to counter objections and remove obstacles.

There are numerous reasons to focus on digital for *Growth*. By far the best reason, though, is the scalability of this approach, and its ability to work for your business 24/7. We will show you how to generate new leads for your team at a fraction of the cost of traditional marketing tactics.

Ask every prospect how they have generated leads in the past. If they say want now them to describe that process. For most companies there is no process — it's totally passive.

Section 2 – GROW Your Business

CHALLENGE:
Finding and hiring great people
You know how challenging it is to find good people today. By all accounts, it's going to get even more difficult to attract and hire in the future. We will show you some great ways to find prospective employees so you can get a head start on your competition.

When we talk to manufacturers, we often hear that they have more work than they can get done because they don't have enough employees. With this in mind, and the reality that in the coming years many predict that hiring workers will become even more difficult, we can share what's worked for a lot of companies. You may already be doing some of these things, but hopefully you can find something in this list that you haven't yet tried.

Well-written job descriptions. Having a well-written job description is imperative in order to find qualified candidates for an open position. There are countless articles and resources about creating great job descriptions. Suffice it to say, if your job descriptions are nothing more than a list of duties, you'll be starting at a disadvantage. In today's job market, your best prospects are probably not out of work but working somewhere else. If you want to access these passive candidates you need to sell them on the idea that your company is a better place for them. Your job postings should provide a compelling story. Share how the job will offer opportunity to grow, how the boss or supervisor will be a cheerleader and how the company has a vision that is exciting.

Placing job postings. Once you've landed on an enticing job description for your open position, you need to post it in the right places. There are many online job boards from which to choose. Most of these third-party websites work well at generating at least some interest. Rather than rely on the job boards exclusively, consider some other ideas that we've seen work really well.

Facebook ads. Run a Facebook ad for your next job opening. Facebook offers employers the ability to target job postings to people with specific job functions at other companies or to people with specific job skills and education that live within a focused geographic area. You can run different ad versions and Facebook's algorithm will automatically determine which one draws the most attention. Once that is determined, Facebook will continue to run only the most successful ad.

Create a video. You may also want to consider creating a video for your YouTube channel, social media and website. Make the video fun and share why working for your company is a great decision for the right candidate. If you are seeking an executive to join your ranks, you'll want a professional quality video, otherwise, there's nothing wrong with producing simple videos using a modestly priced camera.

Post the job opening on social. One of the key advantages of using digital to promote available jobs in your company is the ability for your online community to share opportunities with friends and family. A single post can be viewed by an exponential number of people.

Online diary. Creating an online job diary is another fun way to draw interest in your company. These online diaries help paint the picture of what's involved with a particular job. Typically an employee is selected who has the same or similar job as an open requirement and a desire to share what they like about their work. Each day, the employee spends a few minutes recapping what activities they were involved in. If this approach seems a bit strange, just know that we've seen companies get piles of resumes from people who can see themselves in the job that is depicted.

LinkedIn. Using LinkedIn for research is another great way to connect with prospective employees. If you recognize that most good workers are already employed elsewhere, having a LinkedIn account with enhanced Premium features (which is possible by paying a modest monthly fee) will make it possible for you to contact people, even if you aren't connected.

Pay-Per-Click campaign. If you have a particular niche hiring need that involves an uncommon skill or a geographic location far from your headquarters, you can engage in a pay-per-click search engine campaign to capture interested job seekers. You'll need to create a page on your website or a custom landing page for people to land on after selecting your job opportunity from a search results list, but the investment can reap great candidates in a relatively short time frame.

We know that finding good employees is hard, but we also know that good people are out there. Many of the best candidates are working somewhere else today. If your team diligently uses the online tools and concepts we've outlined, we're confident that you'll find it easier to attract new talent for your company.

1 IN 30

Talk with your HR team and find one action item to embrace. That might be running a Facebook ad campaign or it might be creating a 90-second video highlighting the reasons someone would want to work for your company. Make your video relevant to your desired audience and be sure to include a specific call-to-action that drives interested people to your website. Create a special page on your site that has easy-to-read information in applicable languages, and include a brief first step application form and appropriate telephone number. Then, track your inbound inquiries closely so you can see how your online recruiting efforts bring people to you.

If you're not seeing results, you either have a company reputation issue or you're not running compelling campaigns.

Section 2 – GROW Your Business

CHALLENGE:
Looking at current marketing
Until recently, the return on your marketing investment was quantifiable only by the opinions you chose to listen to. Today, you can know for sure, as modern marketing is quite measureable. Find out what works and then do more of that. Stop wasting money on tactics that aren't bringing you value.

You know the old adage, "Half of our marketing is working, we just don't know which half." This may be true, but it's terrible. If you knew that only half of your employees were working you would certainly figure out which half.

When we say traditional marketing, we are referring to TV, radio, newspaper, billboards, direct mail, tradeshows, etc. Before we discuss reallocating funds to digital, which you know is coming, you should try to understand which traditional efforts are working. You can use digital to do this. For example, as often as possible use a customized URL (web address), phone number or email address on each unique marketing effort. At minimum, do this with each marketing channel. This way you can begin to account for the source of your leads and then assign them to a marketing channel. Relying on your team to ask inbound callers about how they found your company is rarely accurate. The sales team forgets, feels uncomfortable asking or, worse, just makes up information.

Using Google Analytics to see what your new leads are doing once they've arrived on your website will provide valuable information. When you then look at the cost per lead you can make intelligent choices about what changes to make to your marketing efforts. Another option is to ask. Use your social channels or email marketing to informally—or formally via survey technology—ask your consumers if they read a particular trade magazine or attend a specific event to learn more about your industry.

In addition to measuring everything you can, use digital to enhance your physical events, like tradeshows. You might consider placing a kiosk in your booth that gives your visitors a chance to experience your product in some way and then join an email list or enter a contest. The goal is to engage your prospects in some kind of tangible next step. This will help foster a relationship and get them connected to your company. A kiosk today can be as simple as an iPad showing a web page. We are certainly not advocating that you abandon traditional marketing, but using digital you can more accurately enhance what you're doing and gauge what's really working and what's not.

If you do determine that some facet of your traditional marketing isn't bringing desired results, reallocate those funds for some analysis and execution with digital. We will cover some ideas in other chapters, but be assured that your company can purchase a lot of Google AdWords with the budget you're spending on running a year's worth of ads in a lightly read trade publication or using the costs from attending that third most important trade show of the year.

Look at your next event, trade magazine ad or any of the other traditional marketing efforts we have outlined. On your next ad, attach a unique web address and phone number (unique phone numbers are very easy to get). Then work with your internal team or digital partner to make certain that the proper Google Analytics tracking is in place. Establish one measurable goal for interactions from the selected marketing piece and then monitor what happens. If the results are minimal, as they might be, you'll have your incentive to reconsider this channel going forward.

Section 2 – GROW Your Business

CHALLENGE:
Humanizing the brand story
Can your customers and partners tell your business apart from your competitors? If you're looking for ways to differentiate and find customers who are cheerleaders for your brand, you'll want to learn how online efforts can help accomplish this important mission.

Telling your brand story in a compelling manner is a long-term commitment, but with today's modern communication channels it's also easier than ever to do. Let's say that up front. Never before have you had a medium in which you can share your brand story more effectively, efficiently and powerfully. Let's outline how digital can support the communication of your brand.

Understand that your manufacturing company needs to share information about your products with people who currently use your products and prospects whom you want to use your products in the future. If you work with sales channel partners, your goal is to find new dealers and cultivate them. Doing this will help reinforce why your products are the best fit for their customers.

In the past, telling your company's brand story meant running expensive ads in the phone book, newspapers, magazines, radio, TV or billboards. You might have sent direct mail pieces or catalogs to your mailing list of customers and prospects, but because of the high costs involved, inherently these efforts were generally focused more on strong sales language than brand building.

Today, you can bring your company's personality and culture to life by using one or more of the many online digital channels. Not only can you tell your story, you can reveal it by sharing engaging information over a period of time. Best of all, the expenses associated with this kind of marketing are typically modest.

Using your website, Facebook, LinkedIn and YouTube channels, to name a few, you can share your company's story using creative anecdotes, fun photos, infographics and videos. Not only can you tell your story, you can retell it often so people start to think of your company in a positive light. Through pure love of your brand or using engaging contests, you can get customers to share their testimonials and product usage videos.

Because of the flexibility and relative low cost of using digital, you can introduce new products more quickly and begin building interest, even before new equipment is available for sale.

Don't be afraid to have your digital team try new ideas to see what works and what doesn't. As long as you show your business as genuine and not phony, your audience will allow you to make mistakes as you determine how to best use online channels to connect with them.

You can also detail your company's history and culture, something few companies would have been able to afford to do in the past. Funny stories from your organization's past and old photos of founders, employees and facilities are often interesting to your digital constituents.

Another concept we've seen work well is a "meet and greet" website section, where online visitors can interact with someone inside your company. Perhaps you had a "Meet Linda" kind of section in your printed company newsletter, but it was not very dynamic. Allowing your customers, partners and prospects to see the type of people they will work with is a great way to engage relationships between people. It can also be a lot of fun to showcase special interests, historical facts and more.

Let's be clear that sharing this kind of information across social media channels is not free, but with the wide reach of current fans and the possibility of exponential sharing, this method of showing off your company and its people is relatively inexpensive.

A lot of clients we work with are unsure of social media. They often come to us thinking that social efforts are a waste of time. While we sympathize with this attitude, it couldn't be farther from the truth. It may be difficult to quantify specific sales—though not impossible—but this kind of marketing can endear your company to the people you need in order to be successful. When folks see your business as a collection of people doing good things, you'll be in a position to win more business and attract more employees. It may take some time to ramp up social interaction but the benefits can be powerful.

As you go about sharing your story, take time to listen as well. Getting feedback from your constituents can change everything. The "Letters to the Editor" of the past have been replaced by instant feedback. You can monitor comments about your organization, interact with your visitors and find new ways to connect and serve.

Your company's ability to create and share videos rather than using static pictures and text makes all the difference. Whether it is a product demonstration or a culture-centric video about your team, the ease of producing decent quality video today should be amazing to anyone who has been in marketing for over twenty years.

As you think about your brand, remember that it's an ongoing story. In the past, there was no affordable way to produce, deliver and share rich brand information to a large audience. To be effective, you have to make the commitment to continually share your brand story. When executed well, this can be amongst the most successful elements of your marketing strategy, but be realistic about the short-term effect that brand stories will have on your sales. For most manufacturers, this kind of effort is definitely a marathon, not a sprint. Your team should still be able to gauge some key metrics of effectiveness much more quickly than you could have dreamed of ten years ago.

1 IN 30

If your company uses social media and you have not yet produced a video, do so. Do not worry about it being highly produced or the need for it to look like a television commercial. Film a how-to video and make a social post indicating that you have had questions from your customers about the topic covered. If that doesn't meet your needs, congratulate a long standing employee on an anniversary and post it as a sign of stability in your company. A post like this is also a statement to potential employees that you offer a great place to work. Odds are, either of these posts will outperform the average text or image-based post, because people like to see social media content that reflects an organization's genuine personality and culture.

Section 2 – GROW Your Business

CHALLENGE:
Generating more quality leads
Sales professionals always want more leads. We'll give you tips on how to build a steady stream of new leads that can be automatically delivered to the right internal sales team or dealer network.

One of the most common goals we hear from our clients is the desire to attract more *qualified* leads for their sales team to chase. What makes our work enjoyable is our ability to deliver on this need, and often quickly. For most companies, generating good leads isn't that difficult if you follow the appropriate steps. Here's a glimpse of how most companies can leverage digital to generate new leads.

> *Content marketing.* This is a straightforward approach, but very few companies do it and, fewer still, do it well. Content marketing is simply creating compelling information that is interesting to your customers and prospects. The more you write and the more your content is focused on a specific audience or situation, the more leads you will gain. Search engines love content that is targeted to niche topics. Each new article you create is another opportunity for the search engines to index your company and for would-be customers to find you. If you don't have a writer on staff, hire one. Good writers will build a sizable quantity of great content that will attract many buyers over time. The more your information is fine-tuned, the better the chance you will have of showing up in the organic search results when people are seeking the specific kind of products you manufacture.

Focus on Search Engine Optimization ("SEO"). Too many companies leave search engine optimization out of their regular review. It's absolutely mind-boggling. You need to be reviewing how your website—your company—appears in the major search engines. If SEO isn't a priority, you could be missing a staggering amount of potential opportunities to create a relationship with prospects. If we told you that 500 or 5,000 or 50,000 people a month were in your parking lot but couldn't come in (which is really what's happening when you don't monitor and keep your SEO current), you'd surely be upset. Be passionate about SEO because it's a major driver of leads. If you don't have the skills internally to examine your SEO performance and make corrections, hire someone who does. It's critically important to your business.

Strong calls-to-action on every page of your website. You should know that any page of your website can serve as the first page a visitor ever sees. This is because visitors who enter keywords into the search engines see results that can include any page of your public website. With this in mind, each page of your website should have one clear call-to-action. This might be an email newsletter sign up or it could be a quick trade of an email address for a whitepaper on a topic of interest to the visitor. A call-to-action should be easy for visitors to see and perform. Don't make your visitors fill out a long form with required fields to start a relationship with you. Start with a name and email. You can gather additional information later.

Create whitepapers. Whitepapers are short reports, typically 3-15 pages, which detail something of value to the intended audience. Good whitepapers often have beautiful, colorful graphics that help tell a compelling story. They showcase your expertise as a manufacturer and solver of your customers' problems. Whitepapers are a wonderful way to attract leads. If you can capture a visitor's attention with a whitepaper, you can get a relationship started.

Be a blogger. People like to follow others who have interesting information to share. Blogging gives you or your company the ability to share unlimited types of content. You may use blogs to share your industry opinions, your new product innovation process or the good things your company does to promote the local economy. Like other content opportunities, the more finite the topic, the more value you can garner.

Use your social media channels effectively. While we rarely advocate the use of social media channels to blatantly promote product sales, you can build relationships with new people who may be buyers or positive influencers for your business. Create social campaigns that people want to like. In our work, we consistently see that human interest stories win the most engagement. Over time, engagement moves people to reach out. That's when the leads come through.

Offer segmented email newsletters. While many companies have large email lists, few use them well. If you have 30,000 email addresses from customers, prospects and prospective employees, work to segment your list. How? Create newsletter content that spans your various audience needs. Then, using the tools that are included with modern e-mail blast software, move people into different segments based on which articles they click. Over a few email sends you can segment any list into a valuable list of prospects, customers and window shoppers.

Use a company YouTube channel. Using video is a great way to showcase your company and the products you build. YouTube makes it easy for companies to set up their own video libraries. You can even make the content private and accessible exclusively to those with login credentials if there is a reason to do so. In addition to telling a visual story, your public YouTube channel videos will show up as additional listings in the search engines for your business its and products.

Create ongoing digital ad campaigns. You can build online campaigns that convey specific messages to each of your different audience types. For example, if you're looking to hire an individual with specific skills, tailor your message to that kind of person and run it online, where the kind of people you want like to spend their time. Facebook even lets you set up a number of different ads that run concurrently. Then, automatically, the Facebook algorithms determine which ads perform best, eliminating the rest. This powerful testing mechanism helps you determine what messaging works with your audiences for advertising, which you can then apply to your other customer communications too.

Use remarketing. Another type of digital ad campaign is called remarketing. Remarketing is the process of following someone who has visited your website and then displaying a relevant ad for the products they viewed. Learning whether you should display the ad within a few minutes after visiting your website or even days later depends on your business. Remarketing has proven to be a powerful way for companies to gain customer engagement and sales.

Use Customer Relationship Management ("CRM"). In the old days, sales people either kept good notes or relied on their memory to track important information about their customers and prospects. With today's technologies, your sales team can easily track the details of their interactions with customers, prospects, channel partners, influencers and many others. When you connect digital marketing activities with CRM systems, you will gain a new understanding of your sales cycles. This kind of intelligence helps companies fine-tune their sales training, marketing messaging and forecasting.

Set up exclusive toll-free telephone numbers. One of the most interesting things we've discovered is how many companies disregard the web, thinking it isn't that important to them. While it may be true that some companies probably don't need the internet—though that group is shrinking more and more all the time—a lot of companies just don't believe their website does much. That's where exclusive toll-free telephone numbers come in.

In our work, we've discovered on countless occasions that our clients' websites are a critical component of their sales process. Although it may be common, due to the nature of your business, for visitors to reach out via phone, it shouldn't discredit the value of a website. If companies don't survey their callers, they'll never know how important their website is in the acquisition of leads.

Having specialized phone numbers makes it easy to track the quantity and types of calls your company generates from its web activities. Doing this kind of research will help you justify the investment of additional digital marketing activities.

There are several ways in which digital can help you generate more high quality leads faster than ever before. Although not all of these ideas may work for your company, we hope you are able to find at least one that will.

Leads are the lifeblood of your sales team, whether they are internal staff or external dealers. Turn to the search engines for help attracting people who want to buy your equipment. Get with someone who knows how to research Google keywords (Google is the biggest search engine, so start there) and then run a campaign that includes five or fewer keyword phrases that your prospective customers are typing into Google to find products like yours.

Set up a separate page on your website that offers meaningful information with a strong call-to-action and then link that page to your Google AdWords. If you set up your campaign correctly, you'll be surprised at the number of calls you receive—and your sales team will love you for it.

Section 2 – GROW Your Business

CHALLENGE:
Selling more products and services
Nearly all manufacturers want to sell more. If your business is not fully embracing digital marketing, you may be missing out on a lot of potential sales opportunities.

For some of you this may be the most important challenge in this book. We hear this desire a lot from our new clients. If you have a good business but are finding that sales growth has become more difficult than ever, maybe it's because you're up against new competitors, more savvy marketers or, perhaps, your customers are wanting something new and different.

If you approach the process in the right way, garnering more sales using digital is certainly possible. Don't rush into digital marketing tactics before you have carefully researched the landscape of your particular market. You will want to assess what barriers exist that are keeping you from enough new business.

The first step is to understand your customers. We talk about this groups in *Section 1- Run Your Business*. If you haven't read that challenge area, do so before you go any further. More than ever before, you need to really understand your customers. You need to know what drives them, what problems they are trying to solve and how they make buying decisions. Without this knowledge, you could end up spending a lot of money with little return. You also need to know who your competitors are and how they're approaching the market. Once you have a clear understanding of your customers, have developed personas for each customer type and the details of your specific competitive landscape, you can proceed toward success.

Let's get back to the broader concept of growing your organization's sales. We will start with your customer data and then move on to how your company handles the sales process.

You may not realize it, but the most valuable asset your company has is your customer list. In the event of a physical disaster to your facilities, you can always rebuild. Should all of your employees walk out this afternoon, it would surely be painful, but you could rehire and get back up and running. Without your list of customers, however, you'd really be restarting at square one.

Taking this a bit further, do you have a good email list of all of your customers? If you don't sell products directly to consumers, we'll share some ideas about how you can begin building a list of end consumers. With this list, you can start building a relationship with these people that has the potential to bring your business a lot of benefit. Assuming that you do sell your equipment directly to consumers, here are some thoughts about increasing sales.

> *Send relevant email newsletters.* Email is still a powerful method to connect with your current and prospective customers. Too often, we see companies misusing this great communication tool. Unless your business builds and distributes its equipment to one type of customer only, don't send the same email to the whole group. Segment your customer lists into groups of customer types. Then, create content that's relevant for each group. This way, your newsletters will be desirable and read, as the content is worthwhile to the recipient. Another strong caveat is to use an appropriate cadence with your email sends.

> *Manage the email lists.* Managing the lists, building the groups and writing the content may seem like a big job—and it is—but when done correctly, the results are fantastic. You'll have happier, more loyal customers who look forward to hearing from you, buy more products

and are more willing to share their satisfaction about their interaction with your company. Be careful that you don't over send email communications to your lists. If you do, you'll find that a lot of good people become fatigued and will ask to be removed from your list. We see this happen all the time with companies that send too many emails. Don't be the company that loses email addresses faster than you acquire them.

There are several good email marketing software options and most offer similar features. Any of these software companies will offer a free, online demonstration, if asked. Find a tool you like and then get your e-newsletters segmented and on a regular schedule.

Make sure you have a strong call-to-action on your website. Here's a place where many websites fail to deliver. A call-to-action is a prominent next step that you want your online visitors to take. Typically, it's either phoning in a request to the appropriate department of your company (or sales channel partner), or it's a short form that can be submitted to access additional information. The key to success with calls-to-action is to limit each page of your website to *one*. Make sure that every page of your website has an appropriate call-to-action, because with search engine traffic *any page of your website can serve as the first page a visitor sees.* Use a separate web-only phone number to effectively track how your website is serving your sales efforts.

Improve the taxonomy of your web assets. Taxonomy is a fancy word meaning how information on a website is organized, described and displayed. If the idea of getting this done correctly sounds simple, it isn't. The process involved in making this happen is both challenging and one of the most important things a company can do to improve its web success. Whether you're selling products online or working to attract inquiries through your online channels, you either need to have a user experience expert on your team or outsource this effort to a digital agency partner. Doing the research and building a proper taxonomy requires a substantial budget but it's well worth it. The deliverables from this work can be used to inform all of your sales and marketing efforts. When good taxonomy is in place, you will sell more.

Create microsites and landing pages. Somehow, most business leaders seem to think that they can only have one public-facing website. In the battle for online eyeballs, nothing could be further from the truth. Yes, it's reasonable to have a primary gateway website that shares your overall brand story but having specialized web assets, like microsites and landing pages, is a smart way to attract more ideal customers. Microsites are small websites focused on a specific topic, such as an audience, product type or solution scenario. A landing page is a single web page that covers a specific topic.

Imagine your company builds a line of great tires, designed to fit all types of vehicles. A microsite or landing page gets your company associated with the people that use your tires for each specific purpose. One microsite might cover weekend farmers who have small and medium-sized tractors and occasionally need replacement tires. A landing page could be created that provides information about a specific tire you make that's perfect for winter operations.

The primary advantage of these niche websites is a better user experience because, in the example given, the visitor doesn't have to navigate through all of the different types of tires you make; they're able to see highly relevant information that's just about their needs. The imagery, products, voice and tone should all be perfectly matched to this audience. Another big advantage is that the search engines will view and rate this kind of focused content higher when a visitor searches for things like "winter tires for my garden tractor."

Sell into new markets. Another good idea for increasing sales is exploring new geographical markets. One of the great advantages of the digital world is that it offers the potential to open up your business to the world. If you've always sold your equipment into a regional area, there may be opportunities to reach out to new places in the country (or globe) that have the same kind of climate, industry or demographics that your products serve. Digital marketing can be laser focused to highly targeted areas. Because of this, your trial investment in this kind of effort can be relatively modest. Try a few initiatives for three to six months and then, based on your findings, push ahead with what works best.

A/B testing of offers, messaging. The internet provides a great environment to test your organization's messaging and offers. As a small example, Facebook lets businesses set up multiple advertisements within a campaign. The variables can include color scheme, font, message content, promotional offer, imagery and more. Facebook's algorithm then tracks which ads perform best. During a campaign, the most successful ads—those with the highest conversion rate—are then run more and more. This kind of real-time efficiency is only possible with digital marketing and it's incredibly powerful for increasing sales opportunities.

Increase the value of each order. If your business is involved in e-commerce, one of the easiest ways to increase overall sales is adding incrementally to each order. Your grocery store has been doing this for more than a century. They place highly desirable impulse goodies in the checkout line. You can do this same kind of merchandising online. Using cross-sell and up-sell techniques, you can get a percentage of your customers to add additional items to their cart.

The process of promoting additional, related products or services can be done in various steps of your e-commerce process. The actual routines involved in making the online add-on recommendations can be created using automated or manual methods. Related accessory items, special discounts on higher quantities, free shipping and free maintenance can all be offered during the shopping process—at checkout or even after the checkout process. When done appropriately for your products and audience, you should see measureable increases in your per order transaction values.

Experiment with pricing. If you have any flexibility in the pricing of your products, you can use digital to test how changes in pricing, packaging or delivery options are received by your customers. Test your trial prices with a small group to see how they respond before making any widespread changes.

Often, bundling products together can help your organization sell more products, while making it easier for your customers to buy what they need. Other companies find success in selling continuity programs, where customers sign up to receive regular shipments of necessary parts and supplies.

Another usage for continuity programs is having customers sign up for monthly shipments of items that typically come from your stale inventory. You make the value proposition high because the customer is likely getting a lot of value for their subscription fee, but you're clearing out your shelves of dusty stuff that you're close to writing off anyway. This kind of sales concept only works with some companies, but using digital allows your marketing team to get creative.

Consider selling some of your equipment on Amazon, eBay, Google Shopping and Craigslist. Though certainly not for every business, many businesses are finding that these large, aggregate online centers do enable an expansion of sales. There are some things, however, that you need to know before you go down this path. For one, we've seen that there can sometimes be issues with supplier loyalty on the part of these big players. They'll promote your products for as long as people are buying. If orders slow down or a competitor shows up with something better or less expensive, your products can be taken out of the mix with little notice.

Another possible concern is that if your product sells really well, over time these online sales channels may find a competitor to build the products you've been selling at a lower cost, potentially cutting out your business altogether.

Be aware that price is often the only driving factor for many of these online selling behemoths. If your equipment is the least expensive in the category, this shouldn't be an issue. If you're not the least expensive, you may find that it's sometimes tough to get many orders.

Finally, selling through these channels can be expensive and time consuming. Though not ideal for all businesses, selling products via these e-commerce supersites can dramatically boost sales for some.

Sell spare parts online. A number of our clients have strong dealer and distributor sales relationships, so selling assembled products directly to consumers is a no-go for them. Some of these manufacturers have found, however, that these sales partners have little interest in handling "small" spare part orders. These orders typically require a lot of hand holding for a relatively modest order value. Then there's order processing, warehousing of the inbound shipment of parts and the handoff to the customer. It's often just not worth the hassle. This is great news for you if you're willing and able to try this approach. Your margin on selling replacement parts directly to the end consumer should be pretty high. Your team really knows the intricacies of your products and should be able to quickly handle requests and provide accurate replacement part information. Shipping these parts orders directly to the customer saves time for everyone involved.

It's also worth noting that by handling these replacement part orders, your company will be able to collect valuable end user information and perhaps provide better customer service than your sales channel partners.

Sell into non-represented markets. Another option you might consider is selling your products into areas where you don't currently have representation. If you happen to work with sales channel partners, it may be that there are some gaps in coverage. Digital marketing allows you to be laser focused geographically, can yield a high margin and can generate sales opportunities when executed effectively. One of our clients was able to add more than 10 percent of incremental sales to their top line through this one technique alone.

Build social relationships. Social media gets a bad rap from a lot of business owners who think these platforms are for posting trivial pictures of mundane activities. While this may be true for some businesses, successful manufacturers and distributors recognize the value that social media plays in the way people connect today.

Social media, when used as a listening channel, gives you and your team valuable insights on how people view your brand. Social media also allows you to display the human side of your business—your collective personality. Showcase any volunteering or charitable work your team does in the communities where you operate. You don't have to try to sell anything on social channels for them to be a powerful sales tool. Build brand loyalty by displaying that you're more than just a maker of things.

We're not saying that all of these tactics are appropriate for all manufacturers, but it's likely that your company can take advantage of one or two of these techniques to generate additional sales. The key is to measure everything and be ready to pivot as you learn what works best for your business.

1 IN 30

If you're looking to add new sales quickly and are able to invest a minimum of $3,000 each month for the next three months, your go-to action is a Google AdWords campaign. If you can take the time to perform robust research upfront, you'll get better results. We know, however, that sometimes you may not have the time to wait. In that case, our guidance is to limit the campaign to a select geographic market or a refined product or customer niche within your market, and then go after only five or fewer keywords.

With your jumpstart Google AdWords campaign, it's imperative that you get the ad messaging aligned to your target audience, otherwise you will end up wasting too much of your Google budget on the wrong people. Once you have the right message, you need to point visitors to a relevant section of your website or, better yet, to a microsite or landing page that's written specifically for the intended audience. Make sure that wherever you send these Google visitors, there's a clear call-to-action for them. Include your phone number and a brief form they can complete to start the process. Let your visitors choose what action to take but give them a limited choice.

If you follow this approach you should get good results. One important point is that when the inbound inquiries come, your sales or customer service team needs to respond quickly. Often, we find that companies don't get around to sales inquiries until days later. This is not acceptable with digital marketing. Today's visitors expect a fast response. If they don't get it, they may well end up at a competitor that embraces prompt service. If you follow this guidance, we suspect within three months you will have some good new leads to work, if not orders in hand.

Section 2 – GROW Your Business

CHALLENGE:
Expanding market share
Convincing buyers to shift away from competing brands can be done if you have the right messaging and tactics. Learn how companies are using digital marketing initiatives to gain a higher percentage of their total market.

If you want to broaden your business to include new customers, you can pursue one or two primary paths. You can incentivize buyers away from your competition or find people who are first time customers of the type of equipment you make. Either way, you can find solid support from your digital efforts. Here are some examples of how our clients have expanded their market share.

> *Focus on a specific product use or application.* Marketing comes down to presenting a valid message to a prospective buyer in the right way at the right time. If you can focus an idea to a specific niche of your business, you can make the entire message seem more relevant. While it takes additional effort to do this, it can really be worth it.
>
> Imagine a series of landing pages or microsites dedicated to specific uses of your product(s). If your customers use your products in different ways, why not segregate the information about your products accordingly? Having different showrooms to display products might be difficult and expensive in the physical world, but in the digital world it should require far less effort. The power of a relevant message will help you land more customers and help increase your market share.

Try new products, product usages. If you want to have a greater percentage of the market, create new, innovative products, find new uses for your current line or, better yet, do both! Using digital tactics makes it easier for your customers and prospects to get a clear understanding of what you do and how you do it. When that happens, you'll sell more equipment and gain an expanded share of your market.

Combine products into a set. While this idea only works for some organizations, it's a great solution when there's a fit. If you make equipment that comes with lots of ancillary but non-required pieces, consider bundling larger sets of products into a single package. This approach will make it easier for customers to buy your equipment, and often increase your average sale value.

Psychologically, people like to buy what's easiest for them to understand. If your competitor makes customers jump through a bunch of hoops to make a purchase, look for ways to simplify the process. Bundling products into a set is a good way to do this. Try different combinations of equipment to see what sparks the most interest.

Experiment with a better warranty. If modifying your warranty is doable for your business, appeal to prospective customers with an enhanced warranty. This is especially valuable when the products require expensive repairs or long outages when service is necessary. Using digital marketing to put the better warranty in front of buyers is a great way to increase inbound leads for some businesses.

Explore different pricing models. Perhaps the easiest way to increase your market share is to offer lower prices. This may not appeal to most business owners from a profitability standpoint, but growing your portion of the market may mean better service contracts or a more lucrative spare parts business.

In the digital world, you can adjust pricing dynamically, based on whatever criteria you choose. Maybe you want to offer lower prices to customers who are located geographically near your distribution facilities or to all customers during slow periods to keep your factory running at full capacity. Alternatively, you may want to offer lower prices to customers in areas where you have no sales channel representation. Another option is increasing pricing in those markets where the competition is lighter.

The possibilities are endless and the results can help you add new customers. Testing different pricing and other offer options through the many different online channels gives your business the ability to quickly and easily manipulate and measure what works best for your market.

Explore a new market online before you do it for real. In the software business it is very common for companies to produce slick marketing materials that describe software products that don't yet exist. That industry calls this practice "vaporware." The digital world provides the venue for manufacturers to do the same kind of thing.

Your company can display online information about products that don't yet exist. Why would you want to do this? Because you can gauge the interest of a new or enhanced product before your team ever has to build it. You can also try different versions of a product to see what interests your potential buyers the most.

Growing market share always requires diligence, but with the help of common online best practices you can test and carefully measure new ideas in specific places to see what works and what doesn't.

You can gauge interest in a particular product by setting up good digital tracking. You can even create a Google AdWords campaign for a product that doesn't yet exist. Simply create a page on your website that gives visitors an option to provide their email to receive future updates about the proposed product. You might also ask for feedback on what features or functions they would want to see in the would-be product.

At worst, you might disappoint a few people hoping to find a product ready to go and at best, you learn a great deal about interest in the potential product before you engage in expensive product development.

Section 2 – GROW Your Business

CHALLENGE:
Evaluating tradeshow investments

If you are wondering whether tradeshow events are worth their cost, you're definitely not alone. Many companies are challenged by this issue. Typically, most are too concerned to change the status quo for fear they'll look weak to the competition. Learn how some companies are evaluating tradeshows effectively and making appropriate changes.

Tradeshows are one of the most expensive marketing activities many companies still do. In our work, we've rarely seen clients offer much praise for tradeshows. They're really a place to meet up with current clients and show off new products. For some, tradeshows offer the opportunity to gather intelligence on what the competition is up to. Regardless of why you go to tradeshows, the real question is whether the high cost of exhibiting is worth it.

Having attended countless tradeshows over the past 30-plus years, it seems like the following pattern is still the norm today. Each year, as the tradeshow schedule is being set, the sales and marketing team wonders whether it's worth going or not. Inevitably, no one is willing to stop going to shows, though sometimes a concession is made to scale back the booth size or number of team members who go to certain events. Then there's the conversation about what equipment to ship to each show, what new literature is needed and what kind of giveaways are appropriate to lure would-be customers to the booth.

Some venues are especially challenging. The fees associated with transporting and setting up the booth space, getting electricity and internet connectivity can be incredibly expensive. For other locales, the attractions outside the convention hall often draw attention away from the tradeshow event. How many times have your customers and prospects ended up spending most of their "show" time at nearby amusement parks, casinos or great golf courses? It happens all too often.

Now, let's assume that there are ample visitors at the shows in which your company exhibits. Are the visitors engaged and interested to learn about your products or are they wandering aisles in search of trinkets, literature and food to stuff in their bags? When these folks return home, they are bombarded by emails and work that has piled up while away at the show. So what happens to all of that expensive stuff in their bags? It gets stuck in a corner, then weeks or months later, the bags are tossed into the garbage after never being opened. If this isn't a typical experience for you, consider yourself lucky.

We know that some shows are very different, but the above description is apropos for many tradeshow events today. You might have good interaction with your current customers but a lot of prospects would rather learn about your products online than deal with uncomfortable tradeshow chit chat.

If you're still committed to participating in tradeshow events, then at least utilize appropriate digital tactics to get more people to your booth and extend the life of the show beyond the few days of the event itself.

A few weeks before the event, send an invitation to your mailing list and the tradeshow attendee list, if available. Make sure you remove duplications and make the message engaging and compelling. Why should someone visit your booth? Be sure and tailor the email to match the customer's or prospect's interests. In those instances where you can see a good prospect is attending the show, you might consider a special meeting or meal invitation as well. Don't be afraid to combine traditional salesmanship with digital components.

You can create a microsite that highlights the equipment and people who will be representing your company at the event. Again, take this opportunity to encourage people to stop by your exhibit by sharing a compelling story or offering a contest. Getting qualified prospects to your booth and then tracking what happens afterwards is how you determine if the tradeshow expense is worth it.

After the show, create a blog or whitepaper to recap major findings. Doing this will showcase your expertise and give those who attended the show—and even those who didn't—a snapshot of key takeaways.

Make the visitors' time at your booth worthwhile by giving them something that others can't get. Offer an exclusive discount or product bundling to your booth visitors. Create a cool survey and then offer the data or results to tradeshow attendees first.

In addition to taking these basic sales and marketing actions, create buzz by sharing photos of your booth and customer engagement on your social channels. Let your prospects know that you're a great company from which to buy the type of equipment you make. Be the company that does things well and is responsive to customer needs.

Have someone make a video of your company's tradeshow experience and post that to your YouTube channel and link the video to your appropriate website(s). Remember, all of this content will help your search engine optimization too. You'll start to "crowd out" your competitors with this kind of content. Yes, making videos requires some time and a little money, but if you've already made the commitment to attend a tradeshow, creating a video should be a modest addition to the budget and something that will help extend the life of the event well into the future.

Another thing to consider with tradeshows is your associated trade advertising. Many shows have a corresponding magazine or exhibit book in which you can include a print advertisement for your booth. Create one or more unique landing pages to connect your traditional ads with an online element. Put a special web address on your print ad that can be tracked. While it's difficult to track the real value of print ads, it is easy to track the traffic and conversions of landing pages and call-to-action offers.

If your company surrounds its tradeshow exhibition activities with digital initiatives, you will be able to monitor, track and extend the value of the investment. That way, when it comes time to book next year's events, you'll have accurate information from which to make intelligent decisions.

1 IN 30

We know that there may be a key tradeshow each year that you just can't imagine skipping. Okay. So what is the second or third show you are going to this year that probably will cost you more than you'll ever get in return? Quickly put together a realistic cost for attending that show and start with the hard costs. Once you've done this, add up the costs your team has in planning, designing, building, promoting and traveling to this tradeshow event.

If you can stomach the idea of skipping a secondary tradeshow event this year, do so and either pocket the savings or reinvest them in a digital marketing activity. You can look at a more holistic evaluation of your shows, including that one you "can't skip" next year, but this is a great start.

Section 2 – GROW Your Business

CHALLENGE:
Monitoring the competition
Once upon a time, determining what your competitors were doing was difficult or meant a series of covert activities. In today's digital world, keeping up with your competition is easy.

In the good old days, finding out what your competitors were up to involved backroom conversations and even unlawful spying by some. In today's modern world, information about your competitors is available at the click of a mouse. Want to know about their products? No need to send some undercover person to the competitor's tradeshow booth to gather literature, it's all online. Want to know who are your competitors' customers? Check LinkedIn. Check Facebook. Check Twitter. These and other sources will help you see who your customers are courting for new business.

Now some of you might be saying, "Wait a minute! If this is true, why would I possibly want to embrace digital marketing?" While your objection is understandable, welcome to the modern world of business. There really are no secrets anymore. Rather than spending much time worrying about this, beyond running a prudent business, just be an organization that takes advantage of this incredible array of knowledge. The vast majority of companies don't.

Let's take a closer look at how you can effectively monitor what your competitors are doing. Rather obviously, the first step is identifying your competitors. They may be down the street, across the country or on the other side of the globe. Once you have listed your competitors, you'll want to spend some time reviewing each company's website. Some of your more savvy competitors may have microsites that promote specific products or usage scenarios. Make sure you evaluate how those tools are used as well.

If you don't have the competency to review a website from top to bottom and from front to back, engage someone who does. Over the years, some of the most exciting work our team has done involves showcasing a competitor's website from the perspective of learning how they're marketing their products. What we look for are the areas where a competitor's approach and content, including voice and tone, and information architecture are well aligned to the intended audience. As you review a competitor's website, be sure to capture what they're doing really well. Then it's time to look at the mechanics of their website. Is everything being done from a best practices standpoint? Some examples include:

- Strong search engine optimization
- Appropriate navigational structure
- A call-to-action on every page of the site
- Displaying the phone number on every page (ever get frustrated because you can't find a company's phone number?)
- Responsive design that conforms to the type of device being used by the visitor
- Americans with Disabilities Act (ADA) compliance, if appropriate
- Easy to use e-commerce functionality, if offered
- Easy to use dealer (retail) locator
- Links to social media channels

This is a quick list of the basics, but it's a good place to start. After reviewing your competitors' websites you'll want to monitor how each of these companies use social media as well. Also analyze how their key executives leverage this communication channel. You'll probably see a wide range of usage. Some of your competitors may have social media accounts but do little with them. Others will likely have a strong, well-executed social media presence.

Aside from the website(s) and social media efforts your competitors have in place, you can also sign up for alerts from various sources, including Google. This will allow you to see when news, press releases and other noteworthy information is published online about each competitor. Sign up for alerts about your own company and key executives too, if you haven't already done that. It's also good to know what's being said about your team and company online.

Just like your own website's analytics, there are tools that can track your competitors' website and social media performance. Get this information set up for an initial audit and then make it a regular task to recheck. Your competitor's digital activities are fluid. Your competitors may soon launch a new website or social media campaign. If you want to stay ahead of your competitors, you have to review all of these details on a regular basis. It takes time but the information you gather can be incredibly valuable. Besides, your better competitors are watching you closely too.

Once you have a good idea of what's going on in these important areas, you can begin to determine where your competitors are vulnerable. It is within this space where you will find much opportunity to win business and cultivate customer advocates. To make progress you will need to look very closely at your own website(s), assembling the same kind of audit. Be honest. Is your site organized for your audiences? Is there a separate and appropriate experience for each audience type or do you treat every customer the same on your website? Too many organizations set up their websites using their own internal department structure. Don't do this. Think from your customers' perspectives and then build a website that aligns to *their* needs.

In the hundreds of meetings we've had with manufacturers and distributors, we've heard a few ask why they should even play in the digital space if the competitors can follow everything they do. The answer is simple really. The value of playing in this world exceeds the risks. If you want to win in business today, your customers are demanding more and more digital interaction. And, you haven't seen anything yet. In just a few short years, the millennial generation will begin taking over the reins of key buying decisions. As that happens—and it's already starting—your organization will pay a big price if you're not fully invested in digital marketing.

Make sure you have Google Alerts (or other reputation monitoring tools) in place that track your company and your competition. For an immediate impact, see if any of your competitors are on Twitter. If so, it's like an email list with the people's names, titles and businesses displayed. Follow 100 people who are engaged with one of your competitors and see how many follow you back. You will likely be able to gain 10, 20, or more, new followers (leads) who will now see your content as well.

Section 2 – GROW Your Business

more content?

CHALLENGE:
Hiring internal people or a digital agency

Hiring—let alone finding—experienced digital people is a challenge for many. Is it better to hire an internal digital expert or hire an agency? We'll walk you through the options and help you decide what's best for your business.

As founders of a digital marketing agency, we'll share our bias from the outset as we provide guidance to this challenge. We believe that companies are best served by using a qualified, digitally-focused firm to help navigate the digital waters. There is just too much for one, two or even a few people to know. The disciplines required to guide user experience, database layout, programming, responsive design, SEO, ADA compliance, hosting and analytics are vast and everchanging.

Now, we know companies that are successfully approaching digital in other ways. Some choose to have a key marketing person coordinate external activities with various partners, others hire a small team but keep their focus to a minimum number of tactics. In our practice, we've had the pleasure of working with people who really know their craft and many others who are so off-base in their digital mindset that it makes us cry.

So, how should your company move forward and take advantage of digital opportunities? Let's be practical for a minute. Depending on your level of commitment and financial situation, you may not be in a position to put this book down and start doing more than maybe one or two things. You can start the process by identifying something in this book that you think would make sense for your customers, partners or employees. Depending on what that is, you may be able to engage someone internally or hire an outside consultant to perform specific tasks.

Some of the tactics outlined in this book, like developing a comprehensive e-commerce website, intranet or strategic digital campaign will require broader capabilities. For those activities, unless you have a large marketing and IT staff, you'll want to partner with a firm that has a proven track record. Find a group you'd really like to work with and one that's willing to understand your business. While it might be tempting to hire the lowest cost firm, we strongly recommend that you select a partner based on their capabilities and experience.

If you're looking to hire an individual to help manage your company's digital marketing, we recommend finding someone who has experience with digital—not just a marketer. The analytical skills needed to successfully create and interpret digital campaigns are different in many ways from traditional advertising.

Interns are great and well suited to play supporting roles within your digital marketing team, but don't let them operate unsupervised or you'll risk becoming a statistic in one of our future books! While it may seem right to put an intern in charge of your company's Facebook account because they "get" social media, don't do it. Let them gain some real world business experience by working alongside your more senior team members before handing that kind of responsibility to them.

Hiring freelancers is another option that works for some companies. The upside is that you can use these people when you need them and their fees are generally lower than an agency's. The possible downside is that freelancers can get busy with other client work and become unavailable to you at a time when you need them most, or they can get out of the freelance business altogether, leaving your company to fend for itself.

There's no perfect solution. You'll need to figure out what's best for your company. If you have a sufficient budget to tackle some of the larger tasks, having an agency of diverse skill sets will be highly desirable. If your company needs to generate small successes to support further investment, using freelancers may be a better solution. Our final caveat to using freelancers is to pick one who's located in your area. We've seen too many instances where companies were ultimately left with a mess when faraway freelancers stalled projects, became completely unavailable or, worse yet, stole programming code for use on a competitor's project.

Regardless of how you choose to move your company's digital efforts forward, we have one overarching recommendation. Pick people who understand business. The number of people who claim to be great digital marketers is in the millions, for sure. The reality, though, is that while the great majority of these people may know something about how to use digital tools, they don't understand how business really works. That's like hiring someone who knows how to drive a car but can't read a map. They make mistakes because they don't realize how the various facets of manufacturing come together. Don't make the costly mistake of hiring someone who just knows digital tools. Take the time to hire someone (or better yet, a team) who has genuine business acumen.

A final thought about hiring a freelancer or digital agency: please refrain from using RFPs as the mechanism to hire. Interview people or firms and pick the one you like based on their culture, experience and reputation. RFPs are almost always bad because there's not enough information to provide a realistic proposal and, therefore, the budget you'll get back will either be too high, because the responding company is trying to protect itself from what is unknown, or the estimate will be too low because the respondent is okay winning the business and later raising the fees after the deal is struck. RFPs take too much time and effort for all parties involved. You'll be miles ahead if you'll just meet with people or firms until you find one you like.

Create an organization chart for what your digital team should look like in the future. Then assign (only) one major competency for each individual (e.g. "web designer"). If there are gaps between the expertises you need and what you currently have, show the needed capability for each opening but leave the name open. You will likely end up with a chart that reflects seven people or more.

Then prioritize the open seats so you know which one individual is most important to your organization as you begin doing more digital activities. As budget allows, assuming you want to build an internal team, make this person your first hire.

In the meantime, turn to freelancers or a digital agency to handle the activities that are missing in your org chart. Over time you can continue to complete your team by hiring one or two people each year, or you may decide that using an external expert makes more sense for your business.

Section 3
TRANSFORM Your Business

Section 3 – TRANSFORM Your Business

Transform Your Business. Moving beyond the daily business activities that are involved in running a successful manufacturing organization, you may be looking to revolutionize or transform your business into something bigger—or different—than it is today. If you keep up with business and technology news, you know that our world continues to change ever more rapidly. It's likely that a lot of companies in business today won't be here in the future. This is because they aren't evolving to meet the needs of their customers or aren't addressing new competitors who are disrupting long-standing business models and selling new products in new ways.

Talking about *transformation* with our clients is among the most fun we have as business professionals. As a manufacturing company owner or leader, you need to be open to the idea of real change. When you get to that point, the possibilities are enticing. Yes, helping companies automate their data and sell more stuff is definitely worthwhile, but *transforming* business is all about big, new opportunities.

Hopefully you take time during your busy schedule to step back and really think about the future of your business from a 30,000-foot level. When you do get out of the day-to-day distractions, what do you think about? Is creating a viable direct-to-consumer model possible? If you're not already doing business beyond our borders, do you think about doing international business? What if selling the aggregate information you gather every day about your industry was more valuable than the products you build? Think that's not possible? Think again. There are many possibilities to rethink and retool your business model.

You may have thought of some of these ideas before. We are sure that you or your team members have had great ideas in years past. Have you reexamined those ideas you deemed impossible before smartphones were in everyone's pockets? Have you thought about those sacred "we have always done it this way" rules that made sense back then, but are perhaps irrelevant today? It's time to look at your business through a modern lens, and think about how you would run it differently if you were just starting today. Being on this side of the digital revolution, would you operate your business in the same way? Likely not. Let's examine the opportunity to *transform* your business.

Section 3 – TRANSFORM Your Business

CHALLENGE:
Expanding into new markets
If you have capacity and a desire to grow into new markets, we'll share some ideas on how to be successful in your quest.

We are often asked by our clients to help them open new markets. This goal can involve expansion into new geography or adding new equipment to the existing product mix. One of the first steps you can take is approaching the web as if you are *already* in the desired market, well before you actually are. Why is this important? Because you want to see if there are buyers in a particular location for the products you make. Assuming there is a genuine interest in your products, your team can evaluate how much actual sales volume there is and then determine whether it makes sense to proceed.

While discovering that just a few people are searching for something that matches your product offering doesn't necessarily mean there's enough of a market to actually make it worthwhile, seeing a lot of relevant searches in the new market may give you the validation needed to pursue the move more closely.

Using common digital diagnostic tools, it's easy to determine what keywords and phrases prospective buyers are entering into the major search engines to find the types of equipment your company makes. The search terms used can often be quite different based on the geography of the buyer. Almost always, your end customers will surprise you in how they describe your products. Getting a handle on how they think of your products is critical to setting up your business for success online.

You may also look to engage a digital agency or conduct a competitive analysis yourself when evaluating a new market. Once you know what other companies are already selling into the market, you will want to know how they're using digital to promote their products. The analysis should detail the various competitors' websites, indicating what each is doing well and where there is vulnerability. This information is important to have if your company chooses to enter that market. Reviewing a range of available metrics, like search volumes and keyword analysis, you can quickly gather valuable insights on the competitive landscape.

Asking customers and internal team members for their ideas is another great source of product innovation opportunity. It's important that you make it easy for your customers and employees to provide feedback, and that you review it on a regular basis. Some companies offer feedback channels on their website or customer/dealer portals. Other companies choose to offer only an occasional opportunity for this kind of input to happen via social channels or a physical survey. Regardless of whether you have an open door for feedback or just want to gather this kind of information occasionally, the web offers your team the ability to capture and measure different ideas quickly and efficently.

After the analysis work has been completed and you can confirm that your organization still has an interest in pursuing a particular market, we recommend that you turn to pay-per-click (PPC) marketing to further test the idea. Your team or your digital marketing partner can create ads in Google, Yahoo and Bing that display only when the right search terms are entered. The ad messaging should be tailored specifically to the intended buyer. If the online visitor clicks through to your ad, take them to a special page on your website or to a separate landing page that offers additional details about the selected product. If you elect to run campaigns with internal resources, make sure you have someone who knows what they're doing. Running successful PPC campaigns takes know-how or you can end up wasting a lot of money. Without strategic thinking in this area, you won't be able to obtain realistic data. When these campaigns are executed well, the feedback on whether your idea will be successful can occur quickly and without the need for a major investment.

Expanding into new markets or markets that aren't currently served by one of your sales channel partners may mean building direct relationships with end customers. Direct leads can be cultivated and handled by your internal staff, creating both a new market and a high margin opportunity for your business.

In the past, companies may have built new facilities, relocated sales managers and rented office space for sales people to test new market opportunities. These efforts required substantial planning, considerable investment and a lengthy time period to validate the results. In today's digital world, new ideas can be vetted in a matter of days or weeks.

1 IN 30

Pick one new market idea and then create a single landing page that provides applicable details to potential buyers.

Here's an example. Let's say you want to sell a new kind of combination desk/chair set to school districts across the country. To test the viability of this product idea, build a single landing page that has an illustration (or photo if a prototype has been built) of the new product, complete with a full description that's filled with the keywords school purchasing managers use to talk about desks and chairs. Include specifications and pricing if you have that information.

Send an email link to your prospective school equipment buyers. We're assuming you have such a list. If you don't you can use a Google AdWords campaign to drive traffic to this page. Be sure to include a prominent call-to-action so that interested visitors do what you want them to do (call, request a quote, etc.) If you don't get any traction with this approach, it may be an indication that your product isn't yet viable or that your messaging needs further refinement. On the other hand, you may find new sales before you've even ramped up production!

Section 3 – TRANSFORM Your Business

CHALLENGE:
Adding direct-to-consumer business to a B2B model
Transitioning your company to include business-to-consumer opportunities could help you transform your operation into a much different and larger organization. Learn how you can investigate whether this concept is a realistic possibility for your business.

If your business has relied on dealers, distributors, manufacturers' reps or wholesalers to handle the marketing and sales of your products to end consumers, it can be a big hurdle to go after that business directly. Even though many of these organizations are mere order takers, making no effort to actually build a market for your products, they will often balk if they see your company trying to bypass them. This can put your sales efforts in a precarious spot.

So how do you get around this kind of complicated situation? Here are some of the things we've seen work for our clients who have faced this dilemma.

Sell replacement parts online. For many intermediaries, the sale of spare parts is a real pain. There's often a lot of handholding required to determine which part or parts are needed and, typically, the order values are modest. For the manufacturer, however, the prospect of selling these parts directly can be enticing because you already have the customer service capacity and expertise available, and your margin on spare parts is often substantial. Because some channel partners are happy to let manufacturers handle spare part orders, this approach can often be a win-win for all parties involved. The end customer gets the right part the first time, the sales partner doesn't have to bother with small replacement orders and the manufacturer can generate a lot of high margin orders. During this process the manufacturer is also building relationships, directly, with end customers.

Sell only specific products. In addition to replacement parts, we've seen some companies isolate a specific set of products they choose to handle directly. The reasons vary, but most often the products are complex and require engineering or other customizations to fully spec, build and fulfill. The advantage of this approach is your company's ability to test the waters and see how easy it is (or isn't) for your company to handle direct inquiries. If you find that your team can do this well, you may decide that it makes sense to expand the range of equipment offered to end customers.

Handle orders directly in areas where you don't have representation. Perhaps your business has solid sales partner coverage in many, but not all geographic areas. If this is your company's situation, consider selling directly into the gaps. The trick is to make sure that the customers to whom you sell are really located in the defined area and not crossing over from an existing channel partner's territory. This can be resolved by scrutinizing the order's ship-to address or by offering the products at the same price as a neighboring area dealer would. You'll achieve a better margin on this business, as there's no commission to pay. Once you have built up enough business in the gap market(s), you can decide whether to attract a worthy sales partner, giving them a nice book of business from which to start, or continue to take on the business directly.

Create a direct line of products. Another common way to get into direct sales is to create a new line of products that is designed exclusively for the direct market. Generally, these kinds of direct-line products have fewer features and are more economical in price. In this scenario the company's original, higher quality products continue to be sold only through sales channel partners.

If your products can be built with differing levels of quality and features, selling the lower-end versions directly to consumers could be a reasonable way to add incremental sales to your manufacturing business. We've known companies that have been very successful deploying this approach. They especially like having the proactive ability to push for direct sales on those occasions when partner sales are slow.

Sell direct but pay your partner a commission. Regardless of whether your long-term sales strategy includes channel partners or not, you can start with an intermediate step. This concept revolves around marketing and selling your products to your end consumers, but still offering your channel partner in that geographic area some kind of commission or "spiff" payment. This is often seen as a reasonable compromise between traditional selling partners and manufacturers. Making the commission payment to your partner becomes especially important if your equipment requires in-the-field setup or ongoing service.

The various ideas we've outlined for selling directly are viable for some companies. As you can imagine, however, any time a manufacturer displays any interest in selling equipment to their end users, this will raise concern on the part of the channel partners. As a business leader, you need to have an end game in mind. For some, it's simply a matter of time before the intermediaries are reduced or eliminated. For other companies, it's about finding a balance between serving their customers and keeping long-term options open. Still, other manufacturers will never eliminate their sales channel model because they rely on them to handle local maintenance needs or because they've become strong partners that consistently deliver on their promise to build marketshare.

From our vantage point, it's clear that in the future more and more manufacturers are going to start selling their equipment directly to their end customers. Manufacturers will do this because the digital world makes it easier for the connections to happen and because their end consumers actually want to buy directly. If your business can migrate towards this sales approach—even if it's limited to certain products or geography—the transformation of your bottom line can be dramatic.

ask prospects if they might even sell directly to end users.

1 IN 30

Create a short online survey and send it to your end consumers. If you don't have emails for the people who use your products, hopefully you can create a direct mail piece (yes, there are still good reasons for traditional marketing) using addresses from warranty registration records.

Either as a direct question or by drawing conclusions from responses received, determine what services you could offer to your end consumer audience that would be of value to them and add incremental revenue to your business. Take these findings and craft a new service offering.

Section 3 – TRANSFORM Your Business

CHALLENGE:
Exploring international opportunities
Selling products into foreign markets used to require a series of time consuming, often mysterious processes. Today, the internet makes international sales and marketing much easier and far more transparent. Learn how you can evaluate whether going international makes sense for your organization.

The prospect of growing internationally is an exciting thought for many manufacturers, but there are a number of considerations that must be resolved before any serious move in this direction can be made. For example, if your products require special handling, sales engineering consultation to select the right configuration, or on-site set up and ongoing service, you'll probably need to seek local representation. On the other hand, the barriers to selling online have been greatly reduced if your team can easily accept orders and ship your products directly to end consumers in international locations. If your organization wants to test whether its products are viable in the international marketplace, trials can begin in relatively short order.

Depending on your business and past experience with handling international orders, we have some recommendations to help you get started:

Start in Canada. We recommend that you start marketing your products in Canada. Depending on your company's circumstances, your internal team may be able to handle the sales and fulfillment activities themselves or you can seek a qualified sales partner there. Selling your equipment into Canada may mandate some modifications to your e-commerce platform, because of currency, provincial and postal code differences. If you're interested in selling into eastern Canada, you will have to deal with dual languages, as well (English and French). Canada offers a great opportunity to explore international business and gives you the chance to see, firsthand, how the unique processes involved in doing business outside the USA impact your organization. Assuming your team finds success selling your products into Canada, you can then look at expanding into other markets around the world.

Dropdown list of languages or flags. Another way to approach international sales is to create a dropdown list of languages or flag icons that indicate multiple languages on your primary website. As an initial phase, allow visitors who select a language variant to view a single page of information in their native language that directs them to call your home office customer service or a local, in-country sales representative who can speak with them. You can track how many visits and requests come from this page and then decide whether it makes sense to expand the language offering to additional content or provide the full company and product specification information in the applicable language(s).

If the sales opportunities support the addition of more languages, by all means, make that happen. If not, at least you won't have spent the time and energy to translate your content.

For content translation, particularly if you have complex equipment, engage technical experts who are fluent in the native language. Using automated software to translate content into other languages isn't a good idea. Improper grammar and phraseology mistakes are common with these tools, which can make your company look bad to the very audience you're trying to attract.

Conduct a competitive analysis. As you get started with international business or seek to expand into new international markets more broadly, it's a good idea to perform a competitive analysis to see what other companies are manufacturing and distributing into the desired geographical area. As a starting point, perform a Google search on the types of products you offer and see what results are displayed. You'll need to search in both English, which is the international language of business, and the native language for the country you are reviewing. You should be able to quickly see which manufacturers and sales partners are offering similar products. If you think there's an opportunity for your products, you'll obviously want to seek good legal advice in the country you're targeting. Specific standards, laws and specialized government requirements often apply to companies that sell or distribute products into international markets. Consumer laws vary drastically from country to country. It's vital that you pay attention to the legal and regulatory conditions so you don't end up with a big mess on your hands.

Establish a local or regional partner. If you want to avoid selling directly to consumers in foreign lands, another common option is to establish a local or regional partner who can stock and service your products. In this case you may choose to turn over all sales, marketing, fulfillment and customer service functions. Otherwise you can have your internal team maintain some of these functions. Every situation is different and careful testing can help navigate these new waters successfully. Not unlike developing sales leads, some companies seek new dealers by running Google AdWords pay-per-click campaigns and other digital ad promotions that target prospective in-country partners.

Use global internet partners. A number of companies with whom we work leverage global internet partners like Amazon and eBay to sell their products into all parts of the world. It may not be an ideal solution long-term, as the fees paid to these resellers can be high, but the process is easy to manage and using this type of service can get your company into international business within days.

If your company has never done international business, you'll want to proceed at a slower pace to make sure you understand the complexities. If you experience a few bumps and bruises along the journey, don't give up. The results can be very positive for your company. For quite a number of USA manufacturers, their international sales exceed domestic sales. If you've done things correctly, the internet will make it easy for customers to find you and for your team and conduct business anywhere in the world in real-time.

1 IN 30

Invest in the creation of a new landing page that covers one of the products you make. Focus on a specific international market and find someone to properly translate the information into the local language. Offer product uses that fit the selected country's unique siutation. For most markets, you'll want to display product specifications using metric measurements. The more specific you can be with your content, the easier it will be for prospective customers to find you online.

Monitor inbound calls and inquiries to see if it makes sense to expand efforts with additional landing pages, a regional microsite or a full country-specific website.

Section 3 – TRANSFORM Your Business

CHALLENGE:
Adding a subscription model
Adding a subscription model might incentivize your customers to buy your products on a more consistent basis, giving you better visibility of your production needs. Let's look at how you might revolutionize your business model in this way.

Changing your business model goes beyond just digital execution, of course. But the internet can help you and your team research, test and launch new ideas. While you may already have some big ideas of your own, we want to share with you what our clients have learned during our partnerships over more than 20 years.

Consider offering your equipment on a lease versus purchase basis. If you limit your equipment purchase transactions to just selling equipment, you might consider leasing to provide a more appealing option to some of your customers. Having leases in place makes it easier for your sales team to schedule new, replacement equipment when the lease term ends.

Consider creating quarterly or annual reports of data for subscription purchase. If your company gathers demographic information about your customers and how they use your products, you might be able to sell this data. For example, you know that a specific type of equipment needs replacement parts, maintenance and other ancillary inputs to run well. This kind of aggregate data, including timing and product purchase details could be very valuable to other allied and non-competitive companies. Offering this data report as a subscription could lead to a new revenue stream or perhaps even a completely separate business.

Send monthly packages to your end consumers. If your business has excess products that it wants to move on a regular basis, one idea you might consider is creating a subscription-based continuity program. In this scenario, customers receive a shipment of items from your company each month. You can also use this approach to sample prototype products.

This same continuity model can be used for sending replacement parts that are needed on a regular basis. If your customers need new parts every week, month or quarter, consider a continuity maintenance program that automatically ships and invoices the parts on a predefined schedule. For those businesses that can make this kind of arrangement work, it will provide a great outlet to move inventory, create a recurring revenue stream and build a stronger bond between end consumer and supplier.

Non-competitive allies. Another idea you might consider is partnering with non-competitive allies to offer special discounts on products and services to the collective group of manufacturers. Group buying can lead to better discounts and better service for everyone involved. A website can be created to maintain the list of available product and service discounts.

Another version of this model is creating a trusted arrangement where members of a close network of manufacturers and distributors agree to cross-sell equipment and services to each other's customers.

These ideas clearly aren't applicable to every manufacturer, but we want to share some ideas that have worked for companies that have transformed their business models. For some companies, the risks associated with even trying these ideas may seem too great. Opportunity costs and research expenses are just two of the many risks you'll face if you attempt these ideas. This is where digital can help.

By first doing online research and then reaching out to your consumers via social media or email you can assess the potential need and opportunity for any of these ideas, which is far less expensive than using traditional focus group studies. This initial research can also be done more quickly today than ever before. If one of the transformational ideas we've offered or one of your own ideas appears to have merit, start by creating a microsite or landing page that details the new concept to your audience(s). Then, use digital marketing to make your target customers aware of your new product or service and drive them to your new microsite for compelling information and a clear call-to-action.

These ideas for adding a subscription model to your business can all leverage digital marketing to quickly determine whether there's viability for your company. Don't forget that implementing any of these concepts would not have previously been possible, but with digital tactics it's now easier to form an online store, and to market and manage memberships and subscriptions.

Today, you can test and promote ideas and manage the entire process affordably. You don't need to print membership kits or set up physical stores in locations across the country. In the past, these barriers kept innovative ideas like these on a napkin, but now your company can consider and test new sales experiments quickly and easily, knowing that any one of them could transform your business.

1 IN 30

Take one of the ideas that you believe might work for your business and flesh it out. Head to the search engine of your choice and search for your idea. See if another company is already offering the product or service you're contemplating. You can then decide whether to take a chance and put your idea on your company's social media channel to garner traction with your followers. Sure, one of your competitors may see your new idea, but they will likely let all the barriers stop them from mimicking it. Unlike your competitors, you will know if your new idea has the potential to be a hit.

Section 3 – TRANSFORM Your Business

CHALLENGE:
Transitioning to the next generation
Over the next decade, thousands of manufacturing company owners will look to sell their businesses in advance of retirement. Learn how digital marketing can play a big role in this transition process.

There's no doubt that a lot of business owners and leaders are working towards—or worrying about—a major transition to future leaders in the coming decade. If you're wondering how digital can help with this important issue, we're happy to share our experience. We know that this topic can involve difficult discussions, but these tactics can help make the process go more smoothly.

Younger people are more comfortable with digital. Because today's up-and-coming business leaders have grown up with the internet, they're comfortable with it and want to use it in everything they do. They expect to use this medium to access the information they need to make prudent business decisions.

In the last decade we've seen business managers, often family members, go from learners to valuable contributors. These managers are pushing for the changes that are needed to convert old-fashioned manufacturers into modern organizations. Just like the change in manufacturing processes over the past 25 years, business operations are either migrating to modern practices or they're likely on track to die a slow death.

Looking back, we have encountered a lot of younger workers who have been frustrated by their employers (manufacturing company owners), who weren't ready or willing to invest in digital marketing activities. Fortunately, this attitude has been steadily changing and these companies are in better shape for it from a sales and marketing perspective.

Your business will be worth more if you're using digital tactics in the right way. If you're thinking of selling your business, there's almost always a higher valuation attributed to those companies that embrace digital technology. The reasons are simple. Manufacturers that are able to connect online with their constituents will have a greater flow of information, an increased opportunity to sell more products, and the ability to build market share more rapidly. They will also be able to hire more qualified employees. If you don't believe us, talk to a business broker who has experience with manufacturing companies. A modest investment in digital can mean a huge return on investment.

You can solve one of your biggest challenges by embracing online technologies. If you think about the future, when you won't be leading your company, one of your greatest concerns is probably sharing your deep business experience with the new leadership team. Using digital, you can get all of the customer data, manufacturing know-how and processes into places where that knowledge can be accessed, consumed and enhanced by future leaders. Workflows can be created to make certain that business processes are followed and documented. Digital assets can be cataloged to ensure that your historical documents, records and plans are available when needed.

While some of this history may not be deemed valuable by the next generation, there will likely come a time when at least some of it is needed to ensure a smooth transition.

You can keep connected to your business during the transition in ways you never could in the past. We know that it's hard to walk away from the business you've built, grown or cared for, but having a connection to the new leadership using modern online meeting tools can make the transition easier to handle. These tools eliminate the time and expense of travel and make impromptu meetings easy to conduct. In addition to the meetings themselves, you can have access to online reports that keep you in the loop on the business metrics you deem important.

Having a dashboard of key performance indicators that are pulled from the various software tools used in your business will enable you to monitor your company in near real-time and hold your successors accountable for the decisions they're making.

Transitioning your business to the next generation will require a great deal of time and effort. While bringing your business into the modern, digital age won't help solve all of the challenges you face, it is an important step in making sure your company is well prepared for the next generation.

1 IN 30

Talk to an upcoming business leader whom you are grooming to take over your business and ask their ideas for modernizing the business. Find out how they currently view the marketing of your products. See if they have a desire to elevate your business' online activities in ways you haven't thought of.

Manufacturing and distribution businesses today have brought a vast amount of technology to their throughput, inventory and fulfillment processes, but few are leveraging the communication and marketing capabilities that the internet provides. In talking to your upcoming leadership, you'll learn what they view as important when thinking about taking over the business.

About the Authors

We've been business partners since 1996. We started with Spindustry Digital, a digital marketing agency, and along the way have added three other businesses to our portfolio that include a technical training company, an IT and marketing staffing business and an outdoor lifestyle advertising agency.

Interestingly, we both had a similar upbringing, moving a number of times as our fathers were transferred to new job locations. The experience of moving several times has helped us adapt well to the many business opportunities and situations we find ourselves in.

Steve has been married for more than 30 years to his wife, Jan, and has two grown daughters, Erin and Kyra. He graduated from Iowa State University with a degree in Graphic Design and an emphasis in Journalism and Mass Communications. Steve loves to travel and has had the opportunity to see much of the world, both for business and pleasure.

Michael has been married for more than 20 years to his wife, Lora, and has two school-aged kids, Aidan and Alyssa. Michael graduated from the University of Colorado with degrees in Management Information Systems and Marketing. Michael is a serious Star Wars fan and has an enviable collection of several thousand related toys.

For many years we've talked about writing a book to share the highlights of our work alongside several hundred clients. We've learned that the internet provides manufacturers and distributors with incredible reach. We truly love to help companies of all types, especially manufacturers, find ways to improve sales, position their brand, recruit great new employees and so much more by implementing well-designed and well-executed digital marketing strategies.

Prior to starting Spindustry Digital, we worked together for a number of years at an export management company. We served USA manufacturers to build and support international sales. It's amazing how much has changed in the 20 years since we left that business. Back then the fax machine was revolutionary. Sending literature to a distributor in Asia involved expensive courier services that often took days, and phone calls were terribly expensive. Connecting manufacturers with international distributors and end consumers required a great deal of knowledge and effort.

In the 20-plus years we have worked together, we've found some pretty good success. Our companies have been named to the *Inc. 500* and *Inc. 5000* Lists of the fastest growing, privately held companies in America. Based in Des Moines, we were very excited when the *Des Moines Register* named our agency, Spindustry Digital, the #1 Top Place to Work in the state of Iowa in 2013.

We are blessed with many more awards and honors, but the greatest joy we receive in our work is truly the success our clients get with the help of our team's efforts. Working with our client partners makes our time working in the digital world worthwhile and rewarding.

To the continuing advancement of your business in the digital world, we wish you and your company all the best.

Steve and Michael

CPSIA information can be obtained
at www.ICGtesting.com
Printed in the USA
LVHW041129211118
596895LV00001B/1/P